MEN
AND
SEX

M E N
A N D
S E X

——— ◆◆◆ ———

DISCOVERING GREATER
LOVE, PASSION, & INTIMACY
WITH YOUR WIFE

——— ◆◆◆ ———

CLIFFORD L. PENNER, PH.D
AND
JOYCE J. PENNER, M.N., R.N.

OLIVER
NELSON

THOMAS NELSON PUBLISHERS
Nashville • Atlanta • London • Vancouver

Published in Nashville, Tennessee, by Thomas Nelson, Inc., Publishers, and dis-
tributed in Canada by Word Communications, Ltd., Richmond, British
Columbia.

The Bible version used in this publication is THE NEW KING JAMES VER-
SION. Copyright © 1979, 1980, 1982, Thomas Nelson, Inc., Publishers. Scripture
quotations marked NASB are taken from THE NEW AMERICAN STANDARD
BIBLE. Copyright © 1960, 1962, 1963, 1968, 1971, 1972, 1973, 1975, 1977 by The
Lockman Foundation and are used by permission. Scripture quotations marked
The Message are from *The Message: The New Testament in Contemporary English*.
Copyright © 1993 by Eugene H. Peterson.

Penner, Clifford.
    Men and sex : discovering greater love, passion, and intimacy with your wife
/ Clifford L. Penner and Joyce J. Penner.
        p. m.
    Includes bibliographical references.
    ISBN 0-8407-7790-6
    1. Sex instruction for men. 2. Men—Sexual behavior. 3. Husbands—Sexual
behavior. 4. Sex in marriage. 5. Sex—Religious aspects—Christianity. I.
Penner, Joyce. II. Title.
HQ36.P45 1997
646.'96—dc20   96-43236
                                                                    CIP

Printed in the United States of America.
1 2 3 4 5 6 — 02 01 00 99 98 97

To the men in our lives—

Our clients who have trusted us with the inner workings of their sexuality

And their wives who have informed us of the importance of the husband's role in their sex lives

Our dear friend, Dr. Neil Warren, whose enthusiasm has encouraged and skill helped formulate the essence of this book

Our sons, Greg Penner and John Stellato, whose openness and candor have kept us in touch with the men of the nineties

Our friends—

Peb Jackson for his active demonstration of his vision and ministry with men of all ages

Jack Mount for his model of the servant leader to his family, friends, and community

Paul Schultheis for his support in calling us to the meaning of intimacy with God

Roland Hinz for his sincerity in his own life and with us in seeking the truth

Bud Bare for his love and levity, which have lightened tense moments

Our brothers—Dave, Gene, and Doug Buhler for their gift of themselves to Joyce in teaching her loving relationships with men

Eldin Dirks and Jim Martens for bringing maleness into Cliff's female-dominated family

CONTENTS

Preface

In 1995, Dr. Neil Clark Warren interviewed us for his book *The Triumphant Marriage* (pp. 1–5). That interview became the impetus for *Men and Sex*. In his book he writes,

> I asked the Penners for their list of recommendations for any couple who wants to have a mutually satisfying sexual relationship. After 25 years of holding seminars throughout North America, working with thousands of couples on their sexual relationship, appearing on hundreds of radio and television talk shows, and writing all these books about great sex in marriages, the Penners came at my question with tremendous enthusiasm and confidence. Here are the 10 recommendations they have for how to create a great sex life:
>
> 1. The most vital factor in producing a great sexual relationship in marriage revolves around the role of the man.
> 2. The man must move in the direction of the woman's needs.
> 3. The woman needs to learn how to take.
> 4. The woman must be free to lead in the sexual experience.
> 5. The man must progress very s-l-o-w-l-y.
> 6. The man needs to remain flexible, without a set "agenda" for how things are supposed to go.
> 7. Both husband and wife need to be into the sexual process for the pleasure of it—not for the result of it.
> 8. If one of the partners was the victim of sexual abuse during childhood, there must be healing from the trauma.
> 9. Mutual satisfaction is the expectation in every sexual experience.
> 10. It is vital that both partners know how the body works sexually.
>
> I want to make it clear that mutual sexual satisfaction is a goal that every couple should pursue with great enthusiasm. If all couples in North America could spend a few hours with highly competent sexual therapists like the Penners, their marriages would experience a dramatic improvement in this area.

Mutual sexual satisfaction is a possibility for every couple, and you as a man can make the difference. We encourage you to invest in discovering greater love, passion, and intimacy in your marriage and give your sex life a chance to soar far beyond the potential you ever dreamed possible. Your gains will far exceed your efforts.

Sexuality and views toward it have changed over the years. God designed sex to be a vital, passionate expression of marriage. Throughout the growth of the church in the early centuries, sex became a passion to be suppressed. The twentieth century initially was characterized by the fear of sexual passion typical of those early centuries. Then the sexual revolution of the sixties and seventies attempted to liberate people. Unfortunately, the results of the sexual revolution were degrading to the sex God designed, not freeing the expression of sex in marriage.

Today, movements to build the family and to empower men to be men of God with vitality for integrity, the family, the church, and the world are being led by organizations such as Focus on the Family with Dr. James Dobson and Promise Keepers and other groups who focus on helping men be men.

We call you as a man to make an additional promise to your individual integrity and the integrity of your marriage: Commit yourself to read *Men and Sex* and to Discovering Greater Love, Passion, and Intimacy with Your Wife.

Thank you and blessings,
DR. CLIFFORD AND JOYCE PENNER

Introduction

Three weeks before we were married, Joyce graduated from a Baptist school of nursing in St. Paul, Minnesota. Cliff had finished his junior year at Bethel College in St. Paul a few months earlier. During that last summer semester, Joyce took a preparation to marriage class. Sexual adjustment in marriage was a significant part of that class. So it was Joyce who learned and shared with Cliff the positive attitudes and accurate information about sex in marriage from a Christian perspective.

Coming from our German Mennonite homes and communities in the Midwest and in Canada, we were sexually uninformed and naive. The only instruction either of us received from our homes came to Joyce two weeks before the wedding. It was basically three warnings: (1) The honeymoon would be awful, (2) she would be very tired, and (3) she shouldn't let him use her. (She didn't! She used him.)

We believe that the sequence of moving from our naivete to the wholesome instruction, followed by the warnings and the fact that Joyce brought the sexual information to our marriage contributed to our positive beginning and our growth sexually over the years.

The false assumption that men are supposed to be the sexual experts has been accepted as truth and passed from generation to generation. Even at age five, when you were reprimanded for trying to peek into your sister's bedroom, you got these messages: "You're not supposed to do that" and "boys will be boys." In the second grade, you got a similar mixed message when you tried out the use of sexual slang that you had heard from some older guys. In spite of the reprimands, the accepted conjecture was, "He's practicing being a man." In the fifth grade, when the girls were sent to their menstruation class, you were curious and felt left out. You had a funny feeling that they were learning something mysterious that was unknown to you. That couldn't be!

The subtle training of your expected manly expertise continued. At about that same early elementary school age your cousin, who was two years older, showed you the magazines he had stashed in his hideout. That was the first time you had ever seen naked women. You were left with an avalanche of feelings—scared because you were doing something that you weren't supposed to be doing and excited because of the mix of newness and "badness." Those pictures made your gut churn as it had never churned before. You felt that you couldn't breathe even though you were breathing fast. The lump in your throat almost made you choke. It was as if you didn't want to look and yet couldn't get enough. Confusion would best describe those feelings.

As you moved into middle school, real sex education started. You watched "the movie." Then the doctor or nurse talked about reproduction—how eggs unite with sperm and how babies are born. Gross! You could hardly listen. If you were in a class with boys only, you mainly wondered what the girls were talking about. If you were in a mixed group, you couldn't keep from giggling every time the presenter used a sexual word such as *penis*, *vagina*, or *intercourse*. Watching the girls was the other distraction. You wanted them to be looking at you at the same time that you hoped they wouldn't see what a dork you were. You may have been curious about the information being presented, but you pretended to be cool, inferring you already knew. On the other hand, you may have thought it was really stupid to have to know about that sex stuff.

Being in the know sexually was cool for guys. The guy in your class whom the girls liked was the one who seemed to know the most about sex. At least, he talked big. He always had a story about a girl, or he had a sexual joke to tell.

Those junior high school jokes, implying male sexual expertise, were a major source of misinformation about being a man. They sent the message that the *real man* is the man with the biggest penis, he has his way with women, women are putty in his hands, and they beg for more. That was a far cry from how you felt at the junior high youth camp mixer or at the eighth grade graduation dance. But that was the false expectation that was communicated of how men were to be and how women would respond.

Starting senior high school was pretty frightening. The girls all grew up during that summer between junior high and senior high school. You experienced an ever-present self-consciousness. You seemed to be trying to be what you knew you weren't. Fortunately, all the other guys were trying, too. So after a few months you got used to acting like a cool guy; it almost seemed like you.

Quite to the contrary, you may have been one of those guys whose fear was too powerful to allow you to play the game of pretending. You backed away from anything to do with girls—not because you weren't interested, but because you felt awkward. You would rather avoid dating than feel crummy about yourself and encounter the numbing pain of rejection.

Whichever road you traveled, there was certainly one issue you had in common with every other guy—masturbation. Maybe for you, it just felt good. Or maybe it felt good while it was happening, and then there was the flood of shame and guilt after ejaculation. You'd vow you'd never do that again. That vow grew out of one of two opposite beliefs. Either you had been taught that you shouldn't fondle yourself, so you experienced guilt; or you had garnered from your friends that anyone who masturbates is a real loser, so you felt shame. Your peers may have pressured you to believe that masturbation was a sign that you couldn't get the *real thing*—a woman.

The false message that kept coming through was that men instinctively are sexual experts as well as sexual animals: "Go for as much as you can get! The farther you get, the more of a man you are." Even if you were raised with the biblical teaching that you were to save intercourse for marriage, you may have pushed for as much as you could get. You counted on the girl to slam on the brakes. Sometimes you hoped she would; other times you hoped she wouldn't.

After high school, whether working or in college, expectations grew. Making out, getting together, and going all the way were pressures you may have felt directly or indirectly. You were wanting to be the sexual man the world expected you to be, but at the same time your faith and the church were calling you to keep yourself for your wife. The mixed message was more difficult for some to handle than for others.

Some years later you connected with the woman of your dreams. You knew she was the one for you for the rest of your life. The feelings were intense. She may have been your first serious girlfriend or your tenth. If you married her and continued to function as though you knew best, you likely disregarded her personhood and sexuality, and she probably began to lose sexual interest. If you were fortunate, you listened and responded to your wife and her needs. You took the first step to prepare you for a sexually fulfilling married life that is the basic premise for this book.

A couple's sexual life can be wonderfully satisfying when the man learns to listen to the woman, honors her, and serves her by taking his cues from her. The servant leader finds he has the most responsive wife and the most passionate sexual life. The fact is, *the only possibility for a life of sexual happiness occurs when the man moves in the direction of the woman.* That means letting go of many of the false teachings of your early years and connecting with your wife, both because of how she was created and how she was trained to nurture, touch, care, and feel. When a man listens, responds, and lets the woman lead, it is amazing how fulfilling sex is for both the man and the woman.

This book is about discovering greater love, passion, and intimacy in married sex by breaking down the myths about men and sex. It is not a self-help book. We have written *Restoring the Pleasure: Complete Step-by-Step Programs to Help Couples Overcome the Most Common Sexual Barriers* (Word, 1993). It is not a book of creative experiences. We have written *52 Ways to Have Fun, Fantastic Sex* (Nelson, 1994) as a resource to add variety to your sex life. It is not a general handbook on sex for married couples. *The Gift of Sex* is for that purpose. These and other of our resources are described at the back of this book. *Men and Sex* will empower you to make the difference in your sex life with your wife. Operating on the basis of myths about scoring (chapter 1) or doing what comes naturally (chapter 2) may leave you and your wife wondering if there isn't more to sex than what you are experiencing.

It may be difficult for you to take directions even if you are lost. How much more difficult it is to take directions from your wife during sex. Yet sex works better when the man lets the woman direct. Solomon adored and affirmed his new bride and let her lead their physical relationship. Solomon is the model for the truly satisfied sexual man (chapter 3). Christ gave up His rights (His position with God) for His bride, the church. This is the model for a husband with his wife (chapter 4).

As you let your wife lead, she will teach you that sex is something to *experience* rather than something to *watch* or *do* (chapter 5). Sex is not a spectator sport or a performance. It is not a competition. Your worth as a man cannot be tied up in how your wife responds. Your need for her to respond for you to feel good about yourself is bound to put pressure on her, diminish her desire and response, and distract from intimacy. You both lose. As you relinquish these false expectations, you will discover the intimacy you so deeply long for in sex with your wife (chapter 6).

When sex isn't working the way you expected, you may need to look at the twenty-one common pitfalls men make in loving their wives, you may need to refer to other of our resources, or you may need to seek help (chapter 7). Your sex life is just like an automobile; when you keep it serviced, it functions well.

You can keep your heart (and all other body parts) turned toward home (chapter 8). This will not only help you avoid an affair, but also fan the flames of passion in your marriage (chapter 9). You will discover that a vibrant sexual relationship requires work, but that work leads to a lot more fun and a lifetime of passion (chapter 10). And that is what *Men and Sex* is all about.

Now for you women who pick up this book and helpfully highlight it for your husbands, you are vital to our radical approach of promoting that women lead in sex. As you know yourself and are brave enough to communicate what you know, your sexual life will become the spiritual, physical, and emotional symbol of the intimacy you so desire to share with your husband.

After more than twenty years of being sexual therapists and leading sex seminars throughout the United States and Canada, we are convinced that feeling understood, as well as understanding what works best in the bedroom between a man and a woman, will make you dizzy with exhilaration. We hope you find that to be true.

MEN
AND
SEX

Chapter 1

This Isn't the NCAA

Georgetown and UCLA are in the college basketball finals. Georgetown has had an undefeated season and UCLA has had two losses; Georgetown is expected to have a slight edge over UCLA. The players are hyped, the coaches are both hopeful and anxious, and you, having put your dibs on Georgetown, have planned your day around the event.

Every time Georgetown scores, you're off the sofa with excitement. The tension builds as UCLA pulls ahead. You sigh with relief when Georgetown makes one score after another. But you are uneasy again as UCLA catches up. The rules of the game are clear, and you get upset when the referee calls an "unfair" foul against your team. It ends with a tie, and the two top teams in the nation move into overtime and then into a second overtime. By now you are not even sitting. Georgetown scores, the buzzer rings, the game is over, and your team is the winner. You are a winner—your team won!

That night you get into bed with your wife, and you want to be a winner. You don't delight in her as you would enjoy a Boston Philharmonic concert with the sense of soaking in the beautiful music and feeling your soul moved by the crescendos and decrescendos. No, you identify with the Georgetown basketball players, and you go for the game! You try to score.

Your wife's sexual responses are the baskets you make. The faster and more often you get a response, the higher you score and the more your excitement builds. You go for the hot spots—you manipulate and maneuver the basketball so you will score a basket. If there is no response, you get tense and uneasy. You get frustrated and upset when what you think is supposed to work if you play by the rules doesn't work. It doesn't seem fair.

It seems that you just figure out the rules and she changes them. You are not doing that well. You want desperately to win. After all, if you were a real man, you could bring your wife to orgasm, more than one orgasm, or orgasm during intercourse. If you can't, she (your team) is a loser and you are a loser.

> **MYTH:** *Real men bring their wives to orgasm. If you can't, you are a loser and she is a loser.*

SEXUAL COMPETITIVENESS IN THE MAKING

Preschool Expectations

When did this game of winning and losing at sex really start? Your father may have been filled with hopeful pride when at twenty-one months, you could catch the bright green sponge football or were interested in his computer. "He seems so coordinated," he said. Or he may have exclaimed to your mother, "He's exceptionally bright!" The secret hope was that you would someday make the family proud by playing for the NFL or being a rocket scientist or software developer.

Early School Input

A few years later it was T-ball, soccer, after-school kindergarten football, or your own computer. You heard Daddy tell Grandpa on the telephone about your catch, your two runs, your scored goal, or your amazing skill at chess. If your little hockey team was winning, it was great cause for excitement. If it was losing, it was a "bad team," or there was a "lousy coach." If you were winning at chess, you were a hero. If not, the other person was unfair. The message was coming through loud and clear: To feel good about yourself, get praise, and be liked, you have to score, hit, catch, run, block, and rush. You have to win!

——— ◆ ◆ ◆ ———

You learned early to be in the game for the score; to be a winner, you have to score!

——— ◆ ◆ ◆ ———

Think about the difference between what boys and girls did at recess. Most of the boys were either playing a competitive game or wishing they were playing a sport. Some of the girls seemed equally competitive, but many were talking while they played or were into less competitive, more process-oriented activities such as dance or music. Obviously not every boy was into sports, and not every parent was into winning. If you were focused on noncompetitive activities, you still saw the competition around you and either disdained it or measured yourself against it. Even when the girls were into competition, they did not tend to measure their worth by it as much as the boys did.

Junior High Bumblers

If you ever doubt the male-female differences, visit a junior high school campus at the noon hour or supervise an eighth grade party. When we teach sex education on junior high campuses, one of the most common questions from the girls is, "Why do guys behave like such jerks?" What are these junior high girls talking about? The girls are reacting to the pushing, the shoving, the groping, and the grabbing. Guys behave that way with each other, and they're not offended by that. Some behave that way with girls because they are uncomfortable and experimenting with how to be with girls. Even though the bumbling awkwardness is a necessary stage for junior high boys to experience, girls may feel violated by junior high boys' behavior.

High School, College, and Beyond

In high school, some of the boys dropped out of the competition, but they still went to the football games or watched them on TV. Whether you competed or watched, the stakes were high. Swimming and track were timed to one hundredths of a second. In basketball, there were records of baskets, assists, blocked shots, steals, turnovers, fouls, double dribbles, and more.

In college, fewer young men were participants, and those who were had been at the top in high school, so the competitive pressure increased. Your love for sports may have become NCAA football with all the bowl games and March Madness for college basketball. By the time you got married, you may have been hooked. Perhaps your TV watching got you into trouble with your wife. Your heroes probably became the big guys in sports. You likely idealized the ones with the most home runs, touchdowns, goals, or triple doubles.

Competing, achieving, arriving, scoring, hunting, and winning are natural inclinations for men. They are not likely to be any different when it comes to the sexual, romantic part of life. We are amazed at how often we hear the complaint from women: "It really bugs me when I'm cooking dinner or washing dishes and he comes and grabs me sexually."

———— ◆ ◆ ◆ ————

Competing, achieving, arriving, scoring, hunting, and winning
are natural inclinations for men.

———— ◆ ◆ ◆ ————

IS SCORING WHAT IT'S ALL ABOUT?

What is the man going after? What is he trying to accomplish? He is trying to be a winner, and to be a winner, he has to score, and to score, he has to get her parts to respond. The pressure starts in dating. Guys ask each other, "How far did you go?" or "How much did you get?" or "Did you get to third base?" or "Did you score?" The myth is that a boy or a man should push a girl or a woman as far as she will go. The farther he can get her to go, the more of a man or winner he is. Not true! Sex is not about achieving or scoring.

You Don't Win by Pushing for More

Before marriage, the man pushing sexually (obviously, sometimes the woman pushes the man) puts the woman in the role of setting the limits. If you pushed to touch breasts or genitals, over or under clothes, the system was set that she had to draw the line. If you moved beyond what she intended, a pattern was established that taught her to resist. Even when her aroused state allowed her to go along with your nudge in the moment, she may well have experienced sadness and pain after the ecstasy subsided. She felt that she had given in to you.

A man who pushed for more before marriage is likely to continue the approach of pushing for as much as he can get after marriage, yet sensing that he isn't getting what really satisfies. Sex is about relating and not about conquering, achieving, or scoring. The man's goal-oriented approach will not lead to greater love, passion, or intimacy.

———— ◆ ◆ ◆ ————

Sex is not about conquering, achieving, or scoring;
sex is about relating.

———— ◆ ◆ ◆ ————

Goal-Oriented Sex Never Scores

Ultimately, goal-oriented sex does not score. It doesn't even get you to first base. True gratification does not come from how fast or how often you get your wife to agree, to get aroused, to get you aroused, to reach an orgasm, or to have more than one orgasm. When the sexual experience is aimed at a goal to be accomplished, it will leave one or both of the lovers disappointed. When you grab your wife's sexual parts because that feels good to you or you hope to get her interested in sex with you, she will most surely be turned off. In contrast, the woman who is attended and listened to, who feels cherished and adored, who is affirmed and pleasured will invite more touching and more intensity from her husband.

IT'S NOT WHETHER YOU WIN OR LOSE; IT'S HOW YOU PLAY THE GAME

Love, passion, and intimacy are never about winning or losing; they are about how you play the game. In sex, you need to go for the Mr. Wonderful Award rather than the Most Valuable Player.

———— ◆ ◆ ◆ ————

Love, passion, and intimacy are not about
winning or losing;
they are about how you play the game.

———— ◆ ◆ ◆ ————

Learn to Soak in the Process

Sex requires a total shift in attitude from your natural instincts. A woman does not want to be a conquest, a goal achieved, or a win scored. In the realm of touch, it never works to push, force, demand, or take. Women often have to teach men gentleness, tenderness, communication, sharing, and moving slowly. Since the man is never truly satisfied unless the woman is, he has to shift from his results orientation to the process orientation of the woman. He has to learn to soak in the various movements and beautiful harmony of the symphony rather than go for the winning of his team.

———— ◆ ◆ ◆ ————

Since the man is never truly satisfied unless the woman is, he has to shift his results orientation to her process orientation; he has to learn to soak in and enjoy the music.

———— ◆ ◆ ◆ ————

In *How to Satisfy a Woman Every Time . . . and Have Her Beg for More!* Naura Hayden makes the point that many men operate on the "big bang theory," the theory that harder and faster equals better. Nothing could be farther from the truth.

Shifting from scoring and winning to enjoying the sensations of the moment is not easy, even though it is rewarding. "It is natural for us to want to show affection. But for some mysterious reason, we equate tenderness with sentimentality, weakness and vulnerability. We seem to be as fearful to give it as to receive it," writes Leo Buscaglia in *Loving Each Other* (p. 134).

Scoring and winning are not the goals only in sports; they permeate every aspect of the man's world. You might have laid rubber at the stoplight to prove whose car was fastest or been driven to bring home the biggest paycheck or have the position with the most power. Every part of the man wants to win or score big. No wonder it is such a struggle for a man to feel good about himself in his relationship with a woman and in his relationship with God. Relationships require a completely different approach.

Results-oriented sex, particularly when the man is looking to accomplish something with the woman, leads to pressure, demand, self-consciousness, and detachment from the good feelings of the moment. We emphasize a focus on pleasure rather than on stimulation. We do this out of our practice of sexual therapy. We find that as couples learn to focus on the process of pleasure, rather than on the results of stimulation, they feel less demand, and they are not merely satisfied but deeply fulfilled. The concept is very similar to what Christ tried to teach His disciples: If you want to really live your life, you will let go of it; if you want to gain your life, you will lose it! Similarly, if you want to have a mutually ecstatic sexual experience, you will not be trying to have one; rather, you will be attending to mutual pleasure.

> *Then I looked on all the works*
> *   that my hands had done*
> *And on the labor in which I had toiled;*
> *And indeed all was vanity and grasping*
> *   for the wind.*
> *There was no profit under the sun*
> (Eccl. 2:11).

Chapter 2

Does Good Sex Just Happen?

Whether it is *Newsweek* reporting on the yuppie syndrome of decreased sexual activity or *U.S. News & World Report* on "Sexual Desire: Whether it's dull appetite or ravenous hunger, millions of Americans are unhappy with their intimate lives" (July 1992, pp. 61–66), good sex does not seem to be happening a whole lot in America today. Fortunately, according to the *Sex in America* survey, the best sex is happening between monogamous couples.[1] The epidemic degree of sexual dissatisfaction may be the combination of our complex and busy lifestyles and the belief that good sex just happens. Maybe good sex did just happen when Uncle Pete and Aunt Audrey lived on the farm without electricity and no telephone and the house was dark and children were all snug in their beds by 7:00 P.M.

> **MYTH:** *Sex will be most exciting when we let it happen spontaneously and do what comes naturally.*

Recently, we gave an engaged couple a copy of our book *Getting Your Sex Life Off to a Great Start*. The bride-to-be thanked us and said, "We won't read it until later because we want to just do what comes naturally." The young man and woman are in the top 1 percent of the nation in intelligence and education. They were spending time, energy, and money on wedding preparations, home, work, financial plans, and every other aspect of joining their lives together, but they did not want to in any way ruin the start to their sex lives by preparing for the complex joining of their bodies, souls, and spirits. They were a young couple of the nineties believing the same thing Joyce's eighty-seven-year-old grandmother shared with us a number of years ago: "I don't agree with what you are doing [referring to us as sex educators]. Adam and Eve didn't need it, Abe and I didn't need it, and neither does anyone else."

The belief that good sex happens rather than that you can take responsibility for the quality of your sex life seems to be perpetuated by seeing sex happen over and over again between unmarried couples on television shows and in the movies. The couple find themselves attracted irresistibly to each other, so within moments they are having passionate, erotic sex. Every couple wants to have that kind of gut-grabbing sex. And for some couples, good sex does just happen, but for the majority, a lifetime of exhilarating, fulfilling, and nurturing sexual experiences will take deliberate action.

———— ◆ ◆ ◆ ————

Sex doesn't happen;
you make sex happen.

———— ◆ ◆ ◆ ————

With the exception of rape, incest, and abuse, responsibility rests with each individual for both the quality and the quantity of sex. When you operate on the false assumption that sex happens to you rather than that you make sex happen, the tendency will be to have good sex when you believe you shouldn't and for sex to slide into the doldrums within marriage. If you believe that sex is the automatic consequence of passion, you can proclaim innocence by reason of lack of control for sexual behavior outside marriage and wait for the return of that premarital or extramarital passion to keep sex alive within your marriage. Unfortunately, because of the belief that good sex just happens, when it does not happen or it does not continue to be irresistible, you may believe you are no longer in love.

Dr. Lewis B. Smedes describes the different types of love in *Love Within Limits*. In differentiating between eternal agapic love and temporary erotic love, he beautifully explains the basis for why you may equate being in love with sexual passion:

Eros flickers and fades as the winds of desire rise and wane. . . . If eros keeps waning it will eventually die. When the loved one no longer wills to meet the lover's needs, eros dies slowly. When the loved one leaves and does not come back, eros dies for lack of stimulation. When the lover has no more need of what the loved one wills to give, eros dies. Nourished by needs within the lover and the promise offered by the loved one, erotic love has no self-generating power. It is powerful, but it is not a power in itself (p. 133).

His bottom line is, both partners must will to keep sexual love alive in your marriage. When you allow sexual passion to die, you will believe that your love has died because erotic love is human love.

DOING WHAT COMES NATURALLY

We are blessed that our sex life has been delightful and natural from the start. We contribute our ease in sexual adjustment to our similar backgrounds and the preparation for marriage class that Joyce took just before we were married.

In a sense, we didn't just do what came naturally because we applied the knowledge and positive attitudes about sex and practiced the practical suggestions that Joyce received in that class. In addition, her eagerness to share that information with Cliff opened our communication about this vital dimension of our relationship.

We came to marriage with the same naive German Mennonite background and from warm, nurturing homes that promoted a hard-work ethic and the expectation of setting and attaining goals. Thus, we started with the same knowledge base, talked about the new information openly, and had the expectation that marital and sexual happiness was a goal we could strive for and attain. We believe that basis has allowed sex to flow as naturally for us as it has.

If you and your wife came to marriage as secure and confident individuals with healthy views of sexuality, realistic expectations, and adequate sexual knowledge, you may naturally share intense, sexual gratification with each other with little effort to make that happen. You also are uniquely blessed. Healthy couples can have healthy sex by doing what comes naturally.

WHEN NATURAL IS NOT NATURAL

Poke, Grab, and Bumble

There is a bit of junior high boy in every man. You may like to grab your wife's sexual parts. Sometimes letting that little boy in you express himself can be fun for both of you. Other times you may be avoiding the intimacy of a more mature approach because you feel too vulnerable. You may be fearful of rejection, so being silly or bugging her is easier.

Most women strongly dislike being poked or grabbed. You would be better off facing the fears true intimacy can trigger and take the risk to express your desire and affection for your wife directly. The mature acceptance and expression of your sexuality are natural. She may not always want what you want, but that is okay. As you learn to express yourself freely without demand on her, your natural will connect with her natural.

The Sexually Naive Male

We have written in several of our books about the sexually naive man. This man was raised in an overprotective home or for other reasons missed some sexual development and the awkward attempts to relate to girls during junior high, so he comes to marriage not being natural in the expression of his sexuality.

During the genitally focused two- to four-year-old stage of development, a little boy will discover his penis and realize that fondling it feels good. If he is shamed or restricted, his curiosity will be stifled, and he will not learn that his genitals are a natural, pleasure-producing gift God gave him. If he is taught that his penis was designed by God with very special feelings that are private and an important part of being a husband someday, his genitals will become responsibly user-friendly.

As the boy moves into the preschool years, his curiosity will be evidenced in his asking questions about sexuality. His inquisitiveness will be about how babies are made. If he is reinforced for asking and he is given accurate information, he will move on to school-age exploratory play. In his curiosity to discover whether other little boys are made the same as he is and how little girls are different, if he is taught boundaries and given the information he needs through books rather than laboratory experience, he will learn due respect with positive acceptance of his sexual awareness.

The boy will then enter preadolescence, the junior high years, full of hormonal energy. His erotic feelings and bumbling discoveries will take the form of awkward relating to girls. He will notice girls' development, and he may be aroused by it, and he may behave inappropriately. We sometimes refer to this as the poke-and-run or kiss-and-run stage. Junior high supervised group activities of playing "war" or passing oranges without using hands are great grope-and-grab activities that meet the needs of the preadolescent boy so that he can move into the adolescent dating years with confidence. Unfortunately this level of innocence is but a faint memory for many segments of society.

For the sexually naive man, this developmental process was interrupted at some point so that he did not enter adolescence with confidence in dating. He comes to marriage still behaving like the junior high bumbler. For this man, poking, pinching, and grabbing are his natural way of sexually approaching his wife. His natural is not natural at all; it is a turnoff rather than a turn-on to his wife. As she responds to his attempts with irritation, his confidence wanes, and he becomes even less natural.

If this describes you, be encouraged. You will be very responsive to education and training. With the help of your wife and some exercises and new information, confident sexual functioning is only steps away. With new-found competence, your natural will become natural.

WHAT IF YOUR NATURAL AND HER NATURAL DIFFER?

Claudia came to marriage assuming all men really want is sex. She expected her husband to be the sexual pursuer. Robert's mother was the vibrant, aggressive one, and his father was more laid-back and clearly responsive to his mother's advances.

Robert's and Claudia's tension about sex started on the wedding night. She went to unpack her things and get ready in the bathroom, expectant of his pursuit. He relaxed and turned on the TV, waiting for her to come to him when she was ready. She felt unwanted; he was baffled by her hurt and continued to feel inappropriately criticized when Claudia referred to the incident as an indication of his lack of desire in her sexually.

Chris anticipated their wedding night with eagerness to consummate their relationship for the first time. He assumed that he and Angie would start where they had left off. She imagined they would start with all the intense caressing and kissing and fondling they had been doing that made them feel so impatient to move to intercourse. She lay on the bed of their beautiful hotel room in her negligee waiting for him to come out of the bathroom and join her on the bed. She pictured him coming out in nicely pressed pajamas. When he opened the bathroom door, she was presented with his nude body and a full erection. Having been raised naive and with negative messages from her mother about male sexuality, she froze, and they were unable to consummate their marriage for some months.

Your Eagerness Turns Her Off

As Eric, a man we interviewed for our video series, *The Magic and Mystery of Sex*, said it, "I was like a little boy in a candy shop. I just wanted sex all the time, and I couldn't understand why we couldn't do it all the time." A man's sexual eagerness is often his way of seeking love, and it may be difficult to understand why she wouldn't want the same thing. On the contrary, the woman will often feel used by his pursuit rather than loved. Thus, his eagerness will push her away. Men are more likely to connect and experience love through sex; women are apt to want sex as the consequence of feeling loved and connected. Understanding this male-female difference is central to negotiating a pleasing sexual relationship.

———— ◆ ◆ ◆ ————

Men connect and feel loved through sex; women desire sex as the consequence of feeling loved and connected.

———— ◆ ◆ ◆ ————

A woman needs to feel desired, but she also needs room to experience her desire for her husband sexually. If she is always asked before she gets a chance to do the asking, she may respond as an expression of love, but over time her sexual intensity will dwindle. When you're tempted to ask or pursue, try affirming, validating, and connecting instead. Keep her hungry rather than satiated, but not starving.

Your Interest in Her Validates Her

Maureen, another of our interviewees for our video series, talked about her concerns in response to Dan's lack of sexual initiation. She began to worry that maybe he no longer found her attractive: "Maybe he thought I was fat or something." Yet she was beautiful and trim by all external standards.

Claudia became distrusting of Robert and critical and demanding of him in many ways. Her expectations for sexual intimacy with her husband had been shattered. She felt negated as his wife. Her intense reaction made him feel inadequate and pushed him away even more, which, of course, increased her feelings of being invaluable to him.

A wife is validated by her husband's interest in her sexually if that is expressed by connecting with her and affirming and delighting in her rather than by pursuing her body. When your wife feels honored, adored, and cared for by you, your physical interest and adoration of her will be further indications of your love for her. Gary Smalley communicates the need for a husband to honor his wife in his chapter of *Go the Distance: The Making of a Promise Keeper* by John Trent. He writes,

> Honor is at the heart of all loving relationships—with God, our spouse and kids, our boss and co-workers. To honor someone is to attach high value to that person. It's a decision we make regardless of our feelings. When we decide to honor someone, we're saying the person is extremely valuable and important to us (p. 128).

When you fail to communicate your value of your wife and express your sexual interest by focusing on your needs or on her body, she will feel used. We concur with John Gray's assessment that men are motivated by feeling needed; women are motivated by feeling cherished (*Men Are from Mars, Women Are from Venus*, p. 11). We believe that is why men often pursue sex with their wives by expressing their needs; men think women, like they, are motivated by being needed. You can get both your and her needs met if you recognize your differences.

◆ ◆ ◆

A wife is validated by her husband's sexual interest if that is expressed through connection and affirmation rather than pursuit or expression of need.

◆ ◆ ◆

Your and Her Differences

She says:	*You say:*
"All men ever want is sex! They have only one thing on their minds."	"Women are so fickle. They are always changing their minds."
"He never listens!"	"Talk, talk, talk . . ."
"Why does he never remember what I tell him?"	"All she wants to do is shaaaaaaaaare!"
"If he just touched me the way I asked him!"	"She got turned on when I did that yesterday!"
"All I want to know is that he cares."	"All I want is peace."

You like the room cold; she likes the room warm. You'd rather get to bed quickly; she'd rather spend what seems like an hour getting ready for bed. You'd rather she be on time; she would rather look gorgeous and be late to meet you. You get aroused when she fondles your penis; she pushes your hand away when you come into the kitchen and grab her breast or stroke her. She'd love to sit on the couch and have an evening of just kissing; you think, *Why would she want to kiss and get all excited if she doesn't want to have*

So as you embark on the sea of life...

Copyright 1990 Larry Thomas. Used by permission.

sex? You'd like an eager wife; she'd like a caring, nondemanding husband. The list could go on.

There are some hormonal and functional sexual differences between men and women. The longer the time between sexual experiences, the more a man's need for sex and the more quickly a man moves toward arousal and release. Just the opposite is true for a woman. The longer it has been since a couple has had sex, the less is her need or desire for sex and the more time and connection she needs to experience pleasure and response.

◆ ◆ ◆

The greater the time between sexual experiences, the wider the gap between men and women in their sexual eagerness and responsiveness.

◆ ◆ ◆

For women, sex is more of a total person event than a specific genital focus. That is why women need to experience connection and love to feel sexual; men feel sexual when they are stimulated and get aroused. When men and women do not account for their differences, they will miss each other in their approaches. A man will use the approach that would work for him; he will come up to her and fondle her. A woman will plan a romantic evening and talk and connect and then be disappointed if he did not respond sexually. The total body response for women also explains why women vary more from one sexual experience to another and from one woman to another.

Physically, women have the capacity, not the necessity, to respond indefinitely with multiple or sequential orgasms. Most men, however, require a rest period after ejaculation before they can be restimulated to another erection. That may be twenty minutes or twenty hours. Just as a woman's passion can be interrupted, her orgasm can be stopped at any point by either internal barriers or fears or external distractions. Once a man starts his ejaculatory response, he will ejaculate; his response cannot be stopped. If he wishes to delay ejaculation, that control has to happen before he is about to ejaculate.

Men experience difficulty with either getting or keeping erections or ejaculating too quickly; women have orgasmic pressure and inhibition. This is probably because men in our culture tend to be more active during sex than do women, and the arousal part of a sexual response is controlled by the passive branch of the autonomic (involuntary) nervous system; an orgasm is triggered when the active branch of the autonomic system goes into action.

We agree for the most part with Berry McCarthy, the author of *Male Sexual Awareness*, when he says in an interview with Paula M. Siegel that "men are by and large automatic functioners: They come to the sexual interaction already anticipating it, already aroused, and become frustrated if their partner isn't equally ready for intercourse. They measure their sexual satisfaction by quantity rather than quality. Women, needing some interaction to become aroused, are always playing catch-up with their partner. They tend to be much more concerned with the quality of their lovemaking than the quantity" ("Can You Psyche Yourself Into Sex?" *Self*, December 1990, p. 144).

The differences between men and women are both the source of the greatest conflicts and the basis of the most intense intrigue. We think of men as more predictable, easier to please, not as complicated, and more basic. We think of women as the new, improved model. Women were created after men. Women are much more complex, less predictable, and definitely changeable. A woman is like an ocean—always different, ever-changing, multidimensional; the surf, the tide, the roll, the chop, the wind, the visibility all comprise the ocean. And you say, "Why didn't God make women more like men? It would be so much easier." We say, "But how boring!" The combination of male constancy and ever-changing, complex femininity is the key to keeping sex alive over a lifetime of being married to the same person.

——— ◆ ◆ ◆ ———

The combination of male constancy and ever-changing, complex femininity is the key to keeping sex alive in marriage.

——— ◆ ◆ ◆ ———

With every discussion of male and female differences, individuals will find they are the exceptions. Some women identify more closely with the generalizations about men, and some men find themselves clearly more in the feminine camp. That is why we recommend you and your wife learn about your differences. However you go about it, make your differences work for you rather than against you. The understanding of male-female differences is central to resolving sexual conflicts between a husband and a wife and opening avenues of lusty passion within marriage.

ALLOW SPACE TO BE NATURAL

Spontaneity is great if you are happy with the quality and quantity of the love, passion, and intimacy you and your wife are enjoying by just letting happen what happens naturally. For some couples, that works. For most, the anticipation of being together builds quality, and the allotment of time to be together increases quantity.

Anticipation

Remember planning some of your most exciting dates? What made them special? Usually, it was the care and attention to details—making the conditions right—as well as the anticipation of the event. Often the people planning a surprise party for someone benefit more than the person being surprised. The expectation prepares them to be in the mood and receptive to all the various senses and experiences they are about to register.

For a married couple, enjoying a lifetime of exhilarating and fulfilling sex requires preparation. A great sex life is based on more than just bringing two bodies together because each passionately desires the other. Depending on passionate desire works in the movies, before marriage, early in marriage, and outside marriage. It is based on the assumption that sex happens to you rather than the reality that you are the ones who choose both the quality and the quantity of your sexual experiences.

One concern of many couples is how to know if they will be in the mood if they plan for sex. It is a common myth to believe that desire for sex has to precede sexual initiation rather than accepting that planning can prepare your mood. If you wait for your or her feelings, you allow involuntary bodily responses to control your sex life. If you plan the conditions necessary for both of you, the quality and intensity of your sexual times together will escalate.

———— ◆ ◆ ◆ ————

Anticipation, not spontaneity,
is the key to passion.

———— ◆ ◆ ◆ ————

Anticipation allows a woman particularly to meet the conditions she needs to be in the mood for an intimate time with her husband. You can plan to eliminate or at least reduce the possibility of interruptions that will kill passion. Turning off the ringer on the telephone, putting up a DO NOT RING DOORBELL sign, having the children asleep or out of the home, making certain the baby is fed and changed and not likely to cry (although we became convinced when our children were babies that they had an automatic sensor and did not want us to have sex), and taking care of tasks or thoughts that are likely to preoccupy during sex are all ways of enhancing a sexual experience for a woman.

In addition to eliminating distraction, anticipation helps a woman get in touch with her body and her sexuality. Fantasizing about the upcoming event, taking a special oil bath, shaving her legs and bikini area, reading something sexual, remembering past erotic experiences, exercising, and/or meditating spark a woman's sexual energy.

Time

Daily check-ins. Couples who connect physically in some way every day will have sex more often and will enjoy more pleasure. Daily connecting times can happen around leaving or coming home. They can occur after dinner or at bedtime or at any time that works best for the two of you. If daily physical contact is not happening naturally, you as a couple may find it helpful to look at your daily schedules and select a time when you could connect.

———— ◆ ◆ ◆ ————

Couples who connect physically daily
will have more frequent and enjoyable sex.

———— ◆ ◆ ◆ ————

Daily connecting times may be anywhere from five to fifteen minutes or more. During that time, you may enjoy sharing the content of each other's day, checking with each other about your relationship, praying together, reading together, and kissing passionately.

Celebrate your relationship with kisses. Kiss daily. Kiss softly and tenderly. Kiss passionately and warmly. Kiss when you feel sad. Kiss when you feel happy. We see kissing as the barometer to measure the degree of intimacy and passion between a couple. Rarely have we had a couple seek sexual therapy who were still kissing regularly and passionately. Ask your wife how she feels about your kissing. If either of you is not happy with your kissing, take a private evening to teach each other how you like to kiss. Take turns leading; talk and show each other how you like to kiss and be kissed. A good kisser is usually not too hard and not too tentative, not too wet and not too dry, lingers but not too long, uses his tongue gently and playfully but not forcefully. Test how many ways of kissing you know.

———— ◆ ◆ ◆ ————

Kissing is fun, sweet, romantic,
and the essence of passion;
keep kissing!

———— ◆ ◆ ◆ ————

Quickies. Even though we don't recommend five to seven minutes after the eleven o'clock news, functional quickies are a necessary dietary snack to keep most couples on the same wavelength until they have time for a more nutritious delight.

Although in general all sexual experiences must be mutually satisfying, quickies can be for one or the other or both of you. They can include intercourse, orgasm or ejaculation, or none of the above. They never violate; they are engaged in only by mutual agreement. They may give to one more than the other, but they never take from one in a depleting sense.

Quickies can be fun. A quickie can be a nooner, a sunrise special, an at-the-office surprise, or a bedtime sleeper.

Quickies cannot be the sustenance of your sexual diet. You can survive on quickies, but you will not grow; you will stagnate. Continue to weave them in between your complete meals. They add spark and variety.

Regular dinners. We recommend that regular sexual times happen about once a week, or more or less depending on each person's needs. Most couples do best when time is set aside to bring your worlds and bodies together, to pleasure and enjoy each other's body, and to be free to allow arousal, release, and intercourse as desired.

A well-balanced nutritional meal sexually is mutually satisfying for both spouses, occurs when neither is fatigued, and allows time to not feel rushed. Both are active participants, both are free to pursue their sexual desires without violating the other, and both communicate verbally and nonverbally their likes and dislikes. A weekly diet with these conditions will keep a relationship alive and growing.

Smorgasbord. An interesting addition to regular dinners and quickies is a sexual event in which you are free to ask for what you want. Each partner takes a turn choosing favorites from an entire smorgasbord of sexual activities. You might give each other a list ahead of time. You might have a "his" night and a "hers" night. You might take turns being pleasurer and receiver. When you are the one receiving, you talk constantly and invite exactly the touch and the sexual play that you feel like in that moment. Or you might reverse roles and have the one pleasuring enjoy the other person's body in the way the pleasurer desires.

Nouvelle cuisine. Dinners out these days are typically light, delicious visual presentations. They have wonderful flavor. The tastes linger, and you finish the meal satisfied, but not full. Nouvelle sex is much the same. It seeks not so much to satiate but to satisfy with newness, wonderful sensations, and visual enjoyment. It excites and the experience lingers. Create your own new sex as variety from a regular dinner.

Gourmet delights. Although an ongoing diet of gourmet meals would be far too rich, a gourmet delight—and being left with that overfed feeling—is enjoyable every now and then. Gourmet sexual delights would leave little hunger for sex if they comprised most of your sexual diet, but occasionally, a day to totally and fully enjoy each other without limitations can be a wonderfully satiating experience. The only criterion is that it is mutually desired and enjoyable.

Whatever the focus of the time you set aside, be sure to allot time for just the two of you. Our formula for setting aside time for your private relationship—romantic and physical—is fifteen minutes per day, one evening per week, one day per month, and one weekend per quarter. We suspect that a couple who follow our formula for time to connect and care for each other will end up happy and satisfied.

———— ◆ ◆ ◆ ————

*Time allotment formula for a successful marriage:
fifteen minutes per day,
one evening per week,
one day per month, and
one weekend per quarter.*

———— ◆ ◆ ◆ ————

NEGOTIATE A MUTUALLY SATISFYING SEXUAL RELATIONSHIP

When good sex has not happened naturally or you would like to discover greater love, passion, and intimacy in your marriage, we recommend you identify your differing needs, set time aside for the two of you, and negotiate a mutually satisfying sexual relationship. Many times it works best for couples to negotiate in writing.

To begin the negotiation, each write out or discuss how you would like your sexual relationship to be. Indicate how often you'd like physical contact, what type of involvement would be desirable in that contact, who would initiate, what preparation would be important, what time of the day is best, how long your times should last, what activities would be included, and whatever else the two of you would like to include in your plan for sexual intimacy.

Negotiating a sexual relationship may seem a cold approach. But you will be surprised how much warmth can be sparked when two people feel their sexual needs are heard and respected and a plan for the needs is instituted. We are different, unique persons, not only different in our maleness and femaleness, but in the whole being and the personality. It is unrealistic to expect that good sex will just happen naturally without working out and meeting the differences, at least not in the long term.

Great sex within the commitment of marriage requires much more than a natural response to passion. When the initial passion of a new relationship dies down, the transition to a deeply fulfilling sexual life that will last for decades requires making your relationship in general and your sex life specifically a deliberate focus. That transition is most likely when you know yourselves and each other intimately, behave lovingly toward each other, are both trustworthy and trusting, anticipate and plan for your sexual times, and allot time to connect physically on a daily, weekly, monthly, and quarterly schedule.

> *Foolish dreamers live in a world of illusion;*
> *wise realists plant their feet on the ground*
> (Prov. 14:18 *The Message*).

Note

1. *Sex in America* is a 290-page report of the most scientifically accurate sexual study ever conducted in America. Nearly 3,500 adults were randomly selected and interviewed in depth.

Chapter 3
_____

Go Her Way

Joyce just walked by Cliff's desk and said, "This is so much fun writing together!" Working together sparks Joyce, and Cliff benefits, too. Feeling connected, sharing, and communicating are basic to who a woman is at her very essence. She feels loved in the process of uniting.

———— ◆ ◆ ◆ ————

Tenderness emerges from the fact that the two persons, longing, as all individuals do, to overcome the separateness and isolation to which we are all heir because we are individuals, can participate in a relationship that, for the moment, is not of two isolated selves but a union.
—Rollo May, Love and Will

———— ◆ ◆ ◆ ————

Men also have a need for connection, but for most men, it is not a felt need. Men tend to go for the end result and want sex to meet their need for connection; women tend to go for the intimacy because they need connection to want sex. Every person has the need for connection, the need to be loved by God and by others. The longing for intimacy with God and others is a longing of the human heart to fill the sense of loneliness.

Since the need for intimate union is experienced directly by the woman and meets a basic need for the man, we recommend that you go her way.

According to George Gilder's study of men in numerous societies (*Men and Marriage*), men have to be guided to channel their inherent aggressiveness into their family responsibilities and connections. When they do that, they are more successful and less prone to mental and social difficulties. Gilder's opening statement in *Men and Marriage* reads, "The crucial process of civilization is the subordination of male sexual impulses and biology to the long-term horizons of female sexuality" (p. 5). Thus, both husbands and wives will be happier and sex will work best when the husband moves in the direction of his wife.

———— ◆ ◆ ◆ ————

Since a man's need for connection is not felt like a woman's, we recommend you go her way.

———— ◆ ◆ ◆ ————

KNOW YOUR WIFE

The starting point for you as a man is knowing and accepting that to feel loved, your wife needs to feel heard, listened to, and emotionally connected. There is no substitute for the message that says, "I am interested in what you feel, how you feel, and with what intensity you feel it. When did you first feel this way, how long have you felt this way, and what do you think these feelings are about?"

———— ◆ ◆ ◆ ————

To feel loved, your wife must experience being deeply known by you.

———— ◆ ◆ ◆ ————

Learn About Women

Cliff grew up with his mom and dad and three sisters. Having lived with four women, he knew women and automatically understood many of the ways women are different from men. He had never deliberately formulated the dissimilarities, but they were an accepted part of his experience. Joyce grew up with her dad and mom, three brothers, and a sister. Her comfort with male-female differences was also very experiential. If you grew up with limited or no experience with the natural distinctions between men and women, you will have to be deliberate in getting to know about women and how they differ from men.

Spiritual and Nurturing Needs

By nature, women are designed to know their desire for intimate connection with another. Only a woman can have a child grow inside her as an integral part of her very being, her person. When a woman is unable to or chooses not to bear children, a loneliness cries from within her very being. The empty womb can be filled in other ways and the loss can be grieved, but it is a reality that every woman confronts at some time in her life. God made women to be able to spiritually connect with and physically and emotionally nurture a fetus and infant. He made them with hormones that promote nurturing tendencies. God's reproductive design is crucial to the fact that we believe women will crave spirituality and nurturing more than men will.

—————— ◆ ◆ ◆ ——————

By nature, women are designed for
intimate connection.
Go with God's design!

—————— ◆ ◆ ◆ ——————

Accepting that your wife is likely to have greater felt needs for spiritual and emotional connection will reduce the demand you experience to have these needs and free you to respond to her needs on her terms. The ultimate outgrowth of your response to her nurturing and spiritual needs will be sexual intimacy.

—————— ◆ ◆ ◆ ——————

Accept your wife's greater need for
spirituality and nurturing.

—————— ◆ ◆ ◆ ——————

Hormonal Patterns

Hormonal differences between men and women start in the womb. Not only do the X and Y chromosomes determine whether a child will be male or female, but the male hormone testosterone must kick in sufficiently to make a boy a boy. In addition, the way the brain functions in relation to the secretion of hormones in the developing girl is much more complex than that of a developing boy. There are two major hormones rather than one. These hormones, estrogen and progesterone, control many more functions in women throughout life than the one hormone does in men. The female hormones trigger varying emotional monthly patterns, increased flexibility, and nurturing qualities and abilities, such as breast-feeding. The more you can understand about female hormones and their effect on your wife, the more you will be able to go her way.

———— ◆ ◆ ◆ ————

Understanding the complexity of
female hormones
will help you go her way.

———— ◆ ◆ ◆ ————

Emotional and Relational Desires

Although men's and women's ultimate need to relieve their sense of aloneness by being one with God and feeling loved by other human beings is the same, the approach to getting that need for union met is different. Men go for the short-term solution of sex to feel loved and connected. Women's needs are much more emotional and relational. A woman needs to feel cared for; she needs to feel that her personhood is regarded and is more important to her husband than her body. When she feels understood and validated, she yearns for sexual union with her husband. Thus, as George Gilder states, "The man renounces his dream of short-term sexual freedom and self-fulfillment—his male sexuality and self-expression—in order to serve a woman and family for a lifetime." This sacrifice "is essential to civilization" (*Men and Marriage*, p. 171).

◆ ◆ ◆

*Men go for the short-term solution of sex
to feel loved and connected;
women yearn for sexual union when
they experience that their personhood is regarded.*

◆ ◆ ◆

Here's the shortcut I was telling you about.

Domestic Needs

Many women have no energy left for sex by the end of the day because all of their sexual drive energy has been burned up by the tasks of life. Working at a job, keeping up the house, planning and preparing meals, mothering the children, serving at school, having social interactions, and fulfilling community responsibilities can totally consume a woman so that she has nothing left for you or your sexual relationship. Although you help on occasion—or even regularly—she will feel burdened if she is the designated owner of these duties. Taking on some of her list of commitments will take a big load off her shoulders and free some energy to share with you. Why not start with taking out the garbage?

When are you going to take out the garbage?

Learn About Your Wife

Spiritually

Find out what is important for your wife to feel spiritually connected with you. Take leadership in your spiritual relationship if that works for her. If she is the one who is more apt to think about reading the Bible and praying together, decide how you might support her as she expresses her felt needs. On the other hand, if she feels pressured by you spiritually, back off. Find out what her spiritual and nurturing needs are and how you might connect with them. Frequently, a woman will express frustration with her and her husband's lack of spiritual connection by saying, "All he ever wants is sex!" We suggest that she make a deal that every time they read the Bible and pray together, they will have sex.

Hormonally

We recommend that a woman keep a month-at-a-glance calendar separate from her calendar for scheduling life's events. Items to log onto her calendar are the day of her menstrual cycle (if she is still menstruating), an indication of her mood, awareness of her needs, sexual interest, sexual activity and how that was for her, and other issues that affect you, her, or your relationship. It should be her calendar, not your evaluation of her. The most benefit will come when she shares her calendar with you and you participate by making observations that add to her and your awareness of her hormonal cycles. But this can be a sensitive issue. Respect her privacy and avoid being judgmental.

◆ ◆ ◆

*Sensitively know and respect
your wife's personal
hormonal complexity.*

◆ ◆ ◆

Emotionally/Relationally

The feeling stuff is difficult for many men. How can you know what goes on inside her when it isn't easy for you to know what goes on inside you and it doesn't even seem important to you?

You start getting to know your wife emotionally and relationally by deciding to do just that and then consciously doing it. Practice is necessary. Listening and understanding may not be natural for you, but you will be greatly rewarded. Your wife will respond enthusiastically even as you make faltering attempts.

The emotional/relational issues are all about your knowing your wife. She will feel known by sensing that you want to understand what is going on inside her. This may sound like a gimmick, but it isn't! First of all, there is no way you can fake interest over the long haul, and if you try faking, she'll spot it. More important, when you genuinely attend to her, she will find her heart opening to you as she feels loved. And when she feels loved, she will naturally feel more sexually open and interested.

Domestically

Your help with family and household responsibilities will be of amazing benefit to your relationship. You will need the input of your wife in determining what help would most serve her. She may feel that her job is twenty-four hours a day, even though you are concerned that you are already putting in eight to fourteen hours a day away from home. Attend to her feeling of pressure and stress, and communicate yours. Then together negotiate a system of caring for each other that respects each person's needs. She will receive your concern for her well-being as an important expression of your love.

◆ ◆ ◆

When you genuinely attend to your wife,
her heart will open to you, and her
sexual attraction to you will increase.

◆ ◆ ◆

GET WITH HER

Her Personhood

You start going her way by getting with her as a person. This is an all-day, everyday process. This is not something you start at 10:40 P.M. so that you can have sex at 10:45.

Her Sexual Conditions

All persons, male or female, have conditions that are necessary for them to give themselves sexually. Dr. Archibald Hart discovered in his research reported in *The Sexual Man* that not waiting for the right conditions for sex is the main cause of marital sexual problems. Most people have not thought about or defined the conditions. The two of you might enjoy doing that with each other. Conditions include such life circumstances as timing, state of restedness, lack of stress, removal of demands, degree of peace in the relationship, attractiveness, cleanliness, grooming, personal habits, who initiates, environment, personal regard and care, attentiveness, privacy, activities during sex, and many others that either of you might regard as essential to your sexual availability to each other. Defining positive conditions for sex will reduce stress and guessing.

———— ◆ ◆ ◆ ————

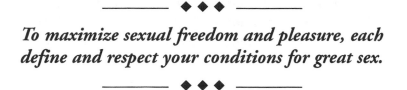

To maximize sexual freedom and pleasure, each define and respect your conditions for great sex.

———— ◆ ◆ ◆ ————

She, being a woman, may have more requirements than you. That may bother you. Men often tell us, "Why can't we just do it? By the time we meet all her conditions, I don't even want to do it." That can be a serious problem. When the conditions themselves become a demand, the conditions need to be negotiated, and the person needing the conditions must take more responsibility for them so that the other's need for relief of demands can be respected. When each person's conditions are negotiated and respected, attended to, and then moved past, sex will escalate to its maximum potential for the two of you.

Her Sexual Triggers

A man often gets triggered by seeing his wife in the nude, undressing, or wearing something provocative. Some women are triggered by seeing their husbands in these ways, but not usually. Women get triggered more by the relationship-emotional-romance behaviors. A look, a touch, a compliment, a kiss given rather than requested, an availability with aloofness, time together, conversation, and pampering are all possible sexual triggers for women. Your wife may know exactly what triggers her sexually. She may never have thought to tell you, or she may believe that if you loved her, you would know. Revealing her secret could be a major change in your sexual relationship. Once you know her sexual triggers, you must not use them to get what you want; rather, respect them to give her what she desires.

———— ◆ ◆ ◆ ————

Respect your wife's sexual triggers to give her what she desires; never use them to get what you want.

———— ◆ ◆ ◆ ————

MOVE IN HER DIRECTION

Knowing your wife and getting with her are only the beginning; the whole sexual experience works best when you move in her direction. This is a radical concept. You may not like the idea at first, but it works and it makes sense. This is the key concept in this book. If you remember nothing else, remember that for the greatest pleasure and sexual satisfaction, the man learns to listen to and follow his wife's lead and respond to her desires. Why?

––––––––––– ◆ ◆ ◆ –––––––––––

KEY CONCEPT:
For the greatest pleasure and sexual satisfaction,
the man learns to listen to and
follow the lead of his wife during sex.

◆ ◆ ◆

––––––––––– ◆ ◆ ◆ –––––––––––

She Is More Complex

The main reason that the man needs to learn to follow the woman is that the woman is a very complex creature. She operates on many different levels at the same time. There is no way the man can keep track of them all simultaneously. That is why he has to learn to follow her lead. We often say that women are somewhat like race cars, and most men are stick-shift Fords. Men may be quite functional and not need as much repair and attending, but most can't compete with women when it comes to complexity and diversity.

––––––––––– ◆ ◆ ◆ –––––––––––

There is no way a man can know and meet
the complex and diverse sexual needs
of his wife unless she guides him.

––––––––––– ◆ ◆ ◆ –––––––––––

When we say that the woman is complex, we mean that in every sense of her being. Her complexity is emotional, hormonal, spiritual, relational, and sexual. She has so much more apparent intensity and variety than the man. Her variety and intensity become evident in the sexual realm with unpredictability and strong reactions that can intimidate and confuse her husband.

A woman's sexual complexity is true in terms of both anatomy and the sexual response itself. Let's look at each of them.

Anatomically, the primary sex organ for the man is the penis; more broadly, the woman's genitals are her primary sex organ. The genitals encompass the clitoris, the labia, the vagina, and other detailed parts. As you look inside the man and the woman, the increased complexity of the woman becomes even more evident. The man has testicles and a tube that carries the sperm and seminal fluid from the testicles to the outside of the body. The Y junction of that tube and the tube from the man's urinary bladder is circled by the prostate gland. The woman has the uterus with its structure and parts, the uterine tubes with their fingerlike projections, the ovaries that produce and release the eggs as they mature, and the upper and lower vaginal canal. The woman's urinary system is completely separate from her reproductive system.

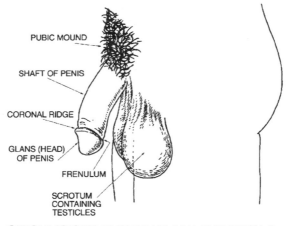

PUBIC MOUND

SHAFT OF PENIS

CORONAL RIDGE

GLANS (HEAD) OF PENIS

FRENULUM

SCROTUM CONTAINING TESTICLES

CIRCUMCISED EXTERNAL MALE GENITALS

Functionally, a woman's sexual response happens on many fronts. Part of the reason that it tends to take a woman longer to get aroused is that she has so many more body parts that need to respond in the sexual experience than the man does. Externally, there are the clitoral engorgement, the changes in the inner and outer labia, and the nipple erection, which are outward signs that would be comparable to the man's erection. Internally,

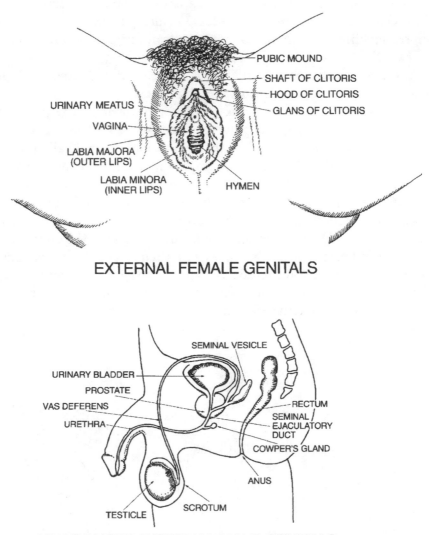

EXTERNAL FEMALE GENITALS

UNAROUSED INTERNAL MALE GENITALS

the woman has even more intricate bodily responses; they include engorgement of the outer third of the vagina, the ballooning of the inner two-thirds of the vagina, the pulling up and away of the uterus so that the penis doesn't strike against it during thrusting, and other internal organ responses necessary for the woman's sexual ecstasy. At the point of orgasm, the woman has two centers of orgasmic response—the vaginal contractions and the uterine contractions.

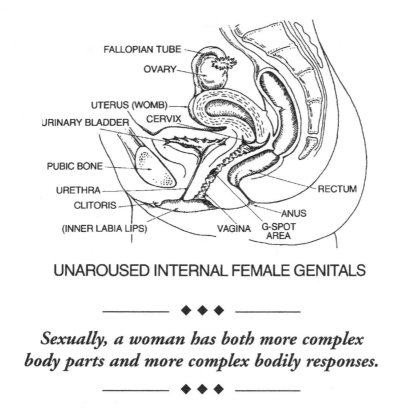

UNAROUSED INTERNAL FEMALE GENITALS

◆ ◆ ◆

Sexually, a woman has both more complex body parts and more complex bodily responses.

◆ ◆ ◆

She Is More Comprehensive

Not only are a woman's sexual involvement and response more complex, but they are more comprehensive. The sexual experience for the woman is a total body and total person experience. Sex is going to be good for her when her husband attends to all of who she is rather than just her sexual parts. According to an Ann Landers survey, women reported that if they had to choose between cuddling and having sexual intercourse, they would choose cuddling. Why? Because cuddling connects with the person.

◆ ◆ ◆

Sex for a woman is a total body and total person experience.

◆ ◆ ◆

She Is More Internal

The male genitals—the penis and scrotum containing the testicles—are right out there, whereas the female genitals are close to her body and covered or internal. The more aroused a man gets, the farther out there his penis protrudes. When a man ejaculates, the product of the ecstasy of his orgasm is the ejaculate, which is expelled away from his body. For the woman, the experience is just the opposite. Even though a woman's arousal starts in response to some external stimulation on the lips, the breasts, the genital area, or the skin as a whole, her response is primarily internal. Even the outward reactions of the clitoris and labia are covered, and as her arousal intensifies, the changes move inward. By the time a woman reaches the point of orgasm, almost no change happens on the outside, and more happens on the inside. The deepest responses of orgasm— the contractions of her uterus and vagina—are reported as pulsations that resonate from within the very core of her being and ripple out in waves to encompass her total body.

She Operates on Two Tracks

Another way to think about a woman's sexuality is to think of it in terms of two tracks. People often say that a man has a one-track mind. Well, a woman has at least a two-track mind, if not a multitrack mind. In the sexual experience, it is natural for a man to be ready for entry and eager to move to the culmination of the sexual experience once he has a full erection. For a woman, physical arousal, although necessary for her to continue, does not ensure readiness to proceed. A woman can lubricate vaginally and have nipple erection within ten to thirty seconds of the initial physical stimulation, yet she may be far from ready to proceed to intercourse or orgasm. That is why we say she operates on two separate tracks. Her body may be physically ready so that entry and intercourse could work well, but emotionally, she is not receptive.

———— ◆ ◆ ◆ ————

For a woman, both physical arousal
and emotional readiness are necessary
for her to proceed to intercourse and orgasm.

———— ◆ ◆ ◆ ————

Physically, the woman has a lot that has to happen to her body before she is really ready to proceed, but even more important, emotionally, the woman must experience the meshing and blending and connecting with her husband before she can feel ready to open herself up to him—to take him inside her and be bound in that deep one-flesh way. This two-track system can be difficult for a man to understand as essential to a woman's sexual experience. Yet if the man is going to be sensitive to and serve his wife and her needs, he will accept that she operates on both tracks. He will know that his wife will not be able to be into the experience with him unless he allows her the time and the conditions for both tracks—the emotional connection and the physical responsiveness.

With the woman's sexual complexity, total body comprehensiveness, internalness, and two-track system of reception and response, it is no wonder that sex works best when the man moves in the direction of the woman. So much richness is added to his experience if he moves in her direction. On the contrary, there is so much emptiness for her if she tries to get in sync with him. When you move in her direction, you will both be ready to proceed to the culmination of the sexual event with a sense of togetherness.

SHE LISTENS TO HER BODY; YOU LISTEN TO HER

Solomon, Your Role Model

You can learn from the greatest lover of all time, King Solomon. As you read through the erotic poetry of the Song of Solomon, you will find a model of how sex works best for a couple. The roles of the husband and the wife during a sexual experience are exemplified.

He Adores Her

Solomon, the bridegroom, talks adoringly about the wonderful attributes of his bride. He compliments her loveliness and lavishes her with praise about every detail of her beauty: "You are altogether beautiful, my darling, and there is no blemish in you" (Song 4:7 NASB). He affirms her. Moment by moment he adores her hair, cheekbones, lips, eyes, and belly. He becomes more poetic, using symbolic language, to describe his enjoyment of her sexual parts. Whatever the words, there is no question that he showers her with praise, with adoration, and with appreciation. He delights in every aspect of her very being—her personhood and her sexuality.

She Invites Him

What does his adoration do for her? It ignites her passion in a powerful way. As she feels adored, she wants him closer. And so she invites him into the tasting of the sexual fruits of her body. The Song of Solomon reads,

> *Awake, O north wind,*
> *And come, wind of the south;*
> *Make my garden breathe out fragrance,*
> *Let its spices be wafted abroad.*
> *May my beloved come into his garden*
> *And eat its choice fruits!* (4:16 NASB).

As she is adored, her breasts swell, her body sends off its fragrance, and her genitals lubricate, and then she invites him to taste of her fruits and drink of her wine. We assume this is meant to be both a literal and a figurative tasting. She invites at her pace and asks for the degree of physical involvement she would like.

He responds to her invitation. The Song of Solomon continues with his response:

> *I have come into my garden, my sister, my bride;*
> *I have gathered my myrrh along with my balsam.*
> *I have eaten my honeycomb and my honey;*
> *I have drunk my wine and my milk* (5:1 NASB).

Whew!

The Formula

The husband adores his wife; as she feels adored, she invites him sexually. His affirmation of her ignites the passion within her.

This is another core concept, the key to a lifelong fulfilling sexual life.

———— ◆ ◆ ◆ ————

The Formula:
The husband adores his wife;
his affirmation ignites her passion, and
she invites him sexually.

———— ◆ ◆ ◆ ————

Think back on the dating days when you were courting the beautiful young woman who is now your wife. You were full of praise and delight, and she was responsive. Her desire for you made you feel great, so you expressed even more positive feelings for her. As your positives fed her positives, she became hungry for more. Within the physical-sexual boundaries the two of you had set, her responsiveness and interest left you deeply satisfied. This positive feedback system in married sex can continue throughout life. As you adore her and she invites you, mutual affirmation will flow.

———— ◆ ◆ ◆ ————

Here is the positive feedback system for married life:
As you adore her and she invites you,
mutual affirmation will flow.

———— ◆ ◆ ◆ ————

Just this past week, we talked with a man who has a national ministry. He goes into situations, senses very accurately and sensitively the pulse of the group or the church, and then connects with them in their situation. As the group encounter his ability to comprehend their circumstance, they move on to greater depth and insight. This is the hallmark of his ministry.

Yet this minister's wife feels very lonely, left out, unheard. As a consequence of his inattentiveness, she is rarely interested in sex. The last time they had sex was about six months ago. In talking with him, we suggested that he practice with her what he does with congregations. We recommended that he empathetically sense what she might be experiencing and communicate that to her. Within three days of making his hesitant steps toward that kind of empathy with his wife, she was inviting him to be with her sexually. Why was that? Because she felt his attempt to hear her and connect with her.

Every woman needs to have the confidence that her husband is genuinely interested in her, her life, and her feelings. Feeling cared about is far better than receiving flowers or chocolates. Then sexual interest follows.

Free Her to Take

As your wife experiences the confidence in her own sexuality that comes from your adoration, she will learn to take sexually. For the sexual experience to be good for both the man and the woman, the woman has to be free to take. When the woman learns to take in touch, take in pleasure, take in arousal, take in passion, sex works best. When the woman is positively selfish, she goes after what she needs. She can know what she needs only as she learns to listen to her body. Her body will let her know when it is hungry and what it hungers for. When she goes for and gets what she needs (not by demand but by invitation), she is happy and you are happy. No one loses! It's a win-win situation.

*You both win when she learns
to listen to her body and go after what she needs.*

You may want a "take" switch that you can turn on inside her body. Like it or not, that switch is inside her brain. If she believes that her duty is to give to you and please you rather than to take, it will require some reprogramming to help her be in the experience for her pleasure and her delight. As she learns to take, she will really give to you; she will give herself and her sexual enjoyment to you. It will take some time to make that shift; think of this as a long-term goal. Over the next two years the two of you will work on helping her to be oriented toward her own pleasure and fulfillment rather than aiming to please you. The result will be that you will be pleased!

Let Her Lead

The Song of Solomon describes the bride leading the sexual experience. She says in 5:3, "I have taken off my robe; . . . I have washed my feet." She prepares her body; she searches for him; she invites his fondling and entry into her body. She is aroused by his adoration of her; she describes her vaginal lubrication (fingers dripping with liquid myrrh) and her body opening up to him.

Let Her Set the Pace

The woman sets the pace in the sexual experience. We have been teaching sexual adjustment in marriage seminars for the last twenty years. Virtually every woman nods enthusiastically in the affirmative when we talk about the need for the man to slow down. As the popular song of a number of years ago emphasizes, every woman loves the man with the "slooooow hands."

Inevitably, the man will move faster than the woman. We teach couples that the man should always keep his pace lagging behind his wife's pace, both in intensity and in activity. A couple helped us picture this by describing how it helped her to not get as fatigued riding a bike with her husband if he always kept his front wheel just behind hers. The same is true sexually. The woman's sexual energy will not fade as readily if the man allows her readiness to set the pace.

◆ ◆ ◆

KEY CONCEPT:
Keep your pace lagging behind your wife's pace
in both sexual activity and intensity.

◆ ◆ ◆

The need for the woman to set the pace and guide the touch is crucial when it comes to clitoral stimulation. Most men are too direct. Most women prefer a more general, light whispery touch that is not on the head of the clitoris but on the hood, stroking the pubic hair, or on the shaft, stroking the inner lips. Since the type of clitoral touch a woman desires can change from day to day or even moment to moment, your wife needs to teach you and guide you. As the man gets aroused and experiences the woman's arousal, he tends to forget what she has taught him and starts to touch her genitally and clitorally with the speed and intensity that he prefers. If you lag behind her in intensity and activity and let her guide you in the moment, you can check your natural tendency to speed up.

As the woman is setting the pace, she is listening to her body, and you are listening to her. How does that work out? First, she has to feel free to both listen to her needs and communicate them to you. You can encourage her to communicate in direct verbal ways and with nonverbal signals. You might start by having her teach you how to pleasure her with the kind of touch and at the pace she likes. She can also guide you in the moment by how she moves her body or how she moves your hands. And as you become more secure, you will take her guiding of your hands not as a judgment or criticism but as a message that she is feeling the freedom to pursue the greatest amount of pleasure. With time and your learning what she likes, she will probably need to guide you less often.

Two experiences can help you learn to listen to her. To do both, you sit with your back against the head of the bed, and she sits between your legs with her back to your chest. In the first one, she teaches you by placing her hands over yours and using your hands to pleasure the front of her body. In the second one, she talks constantly as you pleasure her. It is like she is giving you an ongoing computer printout (a play-by-play account) of what she is feeling and thinking. You can also reverse roles for you to teach her about you. Every couple can create their own version of these suggested learning tools. Once you have tackled the awkwardness of communicating this openly about your likes and dislikes, she will find it much easier to ask for and go after her needs for pleasure during your sexual times.

The Nondemand Position

Touch in Circles

Men tend to touch in straight lines. Women tend to like to be touched in circular motions. The difference between male-female genitals is consistent with this variation in touch preference. The penis is a straight line; the vagina is a circle.

◆ ◆ ◆

Men tend to touch in straight lines; women like to be touched in circular motions.

◆ ◆ ◆

The difference in communication styles is also consistent with difference in touch preference. Men tend to go for the bottom line; women tend to circle into their main point. When Joyce is telling Cliff about an event, a purchase, or a feeling, Cliff usually says, "Just give me the bottom line." That bugs Joyce because her natural way is to tell everything that leads up to and explains the bottom line. She circles in to make her main point rather than goes straight for it. Dr. John Gray also noted this difference between men and women:

> Women enjoy conversation most when they are not required to get to the point right away. Many times, to relax or to get closer to someone, they like to circle around for a while and gradually discover what they want to say. This is a perfect metaphor for how a woman enjoys sex. She loves it when a man takes time to get to the point and circles around for a while (*Mars and Venus in the Bedroom*, p. 35).

When you touch your wife, practice touching her in a circular motion rather than in a straight line. Go with her bodily design. Encourage her to invite circular touching when you most naturally revert to straight stroking.

Limit Same Spot Touching

Don't wear it out! A man has a tendency to stay in one place too long. He finds a spot that works and then rubs it until it is numb. Keep her hungry for more rather than make her want to push you away. It is much better to leave when she wants more than to stay until she wishes you weren't there.

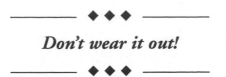

Don't wear it out!

Prepare for Change

What worked last time may not work this time. A woman's unpredictability is a common frustration for a man. Because a man continually looks for some way to figure it out and make it work, the tension bubbles up when the woman doesn't want the kind of touch that produced a positive response the last time.

> ### *You can never know whether what worked last time will work this time.*

Accept this reality for ongoing new discovery as the ingredient that keeps the sexual life interesting. The woman's fluctuations keep the sexual life and spice alive. Her changeableness is another reason why it is essential for the man to follow the woman's lead.

Tease with Promise

Teasing touch has a central place in the sexual experience, but it must be positive for both partners. Teasing cannot be at your or her expense. It should not cause frustration. Rather, teasing touch makes the other person hungry. It is like smelling the chocolate cookies baking in the oven. You can hardly wait to eat them. Part of the enjoyment is the anticipation elicited by the delicious aroma wafting through the house. It is teasing like the contemplation of a wonderful meal, a great concert, or a fun party. It is a promise!

Sexual tease promises to fulfill; it does not withhold. It is similar to circling rather than going straight for the hot spots. You can tease with each other, or you can tease her. You move toward the intense feelings and then back off from them. The intensity of the pleasure will build for both of you if, as you are stroking her body, you move toward erotic stimulation and then move away. As you enjoy touching her body and move toward her nipples, clitoris, or vagina, don't quite go there. Get close and then circle back to more general bodily touching. As you approach the breasts and genitals again, do so with a whisper kind of touch and then back away to enjoy other skin-to-skin touch. The next time you stroke breasts and genitals, use the lightest touch and linger for a moment.

You might pause for ten seconds in the middle of thrusting, but not to frustrate her. If the pause occurs when her wave of arousal has either peaked or dipped, it can incredibly heighten her hunger for more. However, a pause as she is climbing can feel like withholding. The purpose of teasing touch is to allow her to invite more rather than for you to push.

◆ ◆ ◆

Sexual tease promises to fulfill.
It heightens anticipation;
it does not withhold.

◆ ◆ ◆

What We Don't Mean by "Let Her Lead"

We do not mean that you are to be passive or to shut down on your own sexuality. It is equally important that you continue to listen to yourself and express your desires with affirmation and without demand. The woman leading does not give her permission to be uncaring about you. Her sensitivity in leading is just as important as your sensitivity in allowing her to lead. Her leading has to do with setting the pace, learning to take, and pursuing her sexuality with you.

TO BE GREAT, SEX MUST BE AS GOOD FOR HER AS IT IS FOR YOU

How can sex be as good for her as it is for you? She cannot be focused on pleasing you. Her focus on pleasing you will always speed up the process and bypass the intense buildup of pleasure available for both of you. Since the woman's sexual experience is so internal, for her to be externally oriented toward your pleasure will limit her freedom of sexual abandonment and thus the joy and pleasure you both experience.

As you adore your wife, delight in her, talk to her, touch her, and move at her pace, she will begin to experience the longing of her heart. As her intimacy needs are fulfilled, she will open up to receive and respond to you in ways that will make sex with your wife better than you had ever imagined. Emotional intimacy is the precondition to joyful sexual intimacy. Of course, sex without intimacy is possible. Sex with prostitutes or with videos is sex without intimacy. Sex that brings two people together in a deep, lifelong bond of love, passion, and intimacy is found only in marriage.

The message is that great sex has to be as good for her as it is for you. When she has learned to take and you have learned to enjoy the pleasure of loving and serving and giving, then she indeed will experience the deep delights of a fulfilling sexual life, and you will experience the satisfaction and joy that come not only from your sexual fulfillment but also from knowing that sex is every bit as good for her as it is for you. If you doubt this, try it for a couple of months.

> *A wise heart takes orders;*
>   *an empty head will come unglued*
> (Prov. 10:8, *The Message*).

Chapter 4

Your Rights: Are Hers Yours?

An assumption sometimes misused by a man is that when he marries, his wife's body becomes his to possess. An extreme example of this belief is evident from a *Los Angeles Times* interview (February 5, 1996):

> When Ramiro Espinosa used a butter knife to unlock the door to his wife's attic bedroom two years ago and then demanded sex from her, he figured he had the Catholic Church on his side.
>
> But when he tried to use that as a defense last week against charges of attempted rape and spousal abuse, it didn't quite work. Catholic officials said he was wrong and a judge sentenced him to a year in County Jail.
>
> "People have been dragging religion into the bedroom for eons," say sexual therapists Clifford and Joyce Penner, who are sometimes known as "the Christian Masters and Johnson."
>
> "In the New Testament, the debate usually centers around a passage in the apostle Paul's first letter to the Corinthians: 'The husband and wife should fulfill their conjugal obligations toward each other. A wife's body does not belong to her alone, but also to her husband, and the husband's body to his wife. Do not deprive one another.'"

YOU GIVE HER YOURS; SHE GIVES YOU HERS

The instructions for living presented in the Scriptures are written for each person to apply to his or her life. How natural it is, however, to use the guidelines to evaluate, judge, and demand from others. You may have used 1 Corinthians 7:3–5 to demand your sexual rights or, at least, to instill guilt in your wife for not fulfilling her "wifely Christian duty."

Eugene Peterson's paraphrase of 1 Corinthians 7 is refreshing:

Now, getting down to the questions you asked in your letter to me. First, is it a good thing to have sexual relations? Certainly—but only within a certain context. It's good for a man to have a wife, and for a woman to have a husband. Sexual drives are strong, but marriage is strong enough to contain them and provide for a balanced and fulfilling sexual life in a world of sexual disorder. The marriage bed must be a place of mutuality. . . . Marriage is not a place to "stand up for your rights." Marriage is a decision to serve the other, whether in bed or out (vv. 1–4, *The Message*).

A married couple can most clearly exemplify the symbolism between the husband-wife relationship and Christ and the church through their sexual relationship. Each has a responsibility to the other to allow the other to find sexual fulfillment. The best way to achieve that fulfillment is to realize that your body is not just yours sexually; it is also your spouse's. So don't withhold yourselves. Give yourselves freely to each other as Christ gave Himself for the church and wants the church to give itself to Him. Use the instruction in that passage as guidance for what you can do to make your sexual relationship in marriage better, not what God wants your spouse to do. The instruction is to each person, not to use as a demand or threat with your spouse.

◆ ◆ ◆

Just as giving your body to your spouse to enjoy is most delightful, demanding rights to have the other's body is most stifling.

◆ ◆ ◆

As each of you learns to freely allow your body to be enjoyed by your spouse and to enjoy your spouse's body for your pleasure without violation or demand, your sexual relationship will flow freely. You will both fulfill your sexual duty without feeling the pressure that the word *duty* usually elicits.

———— ◆ ◆ ◆ ————

*Each of you has the responsibility to allow
the other to find sexual fulfillment.*

———— ◆ ◆ ◆ ————

This is a two-way system reflected by a spirit of mutuality and respect: You give her your body, and you enjoy hers to the extent that she is able to give hers. Of course, her goal is to do the same with you, but that is her responsibility, not yours. You are responsible for the pleasure you are able to give and receive in any sexual experience with your wife, and she is responsible for the pleasure she is able to give and receive.

———— ◆ ◆ ◆ ————

*Each of you is responsible for the
pleasure you are able to give and receive
in any sexual experience.*

———— ◆ ◆ ◆ ————

LOVE YOUR WIFE AS CHRIST LOVED THE CHURCH

The model a husband can emulate is the model of Christ to the church. That is a high calling. How do you, a human being, love your wife as Christ, a divine being, was able to love the church? The apostle Paul has these words of encouragement: "Not that I have already obtained it, or have already become perfect, but I press on in order that I may lay hold of that for which also I was laid hold of by Christ Jesus. Brethren, I do not regard myself as having laid hold of it yet; but one thing I do: forgetting what lies behind and reaching forward to what lies ahead, I press on toward the goal for the prize of the upward call of God in Christ Jesus" (Phil. 3:12–14 NASB). Even though you cannot perfectly love your wife as Christ loved the church, the goal gives you a standard to work toward.

Servant Headship

You are the head of your wife, just as Christ is the head of the church. This concept of headship is laid out in the apostle Paul's book to the Ephesians. The fifth chapter begins with instructions to all of God's children to be imitators of Him. It then lists ways of imitating Him by walking in love, not engaging in immorality or impurity, not deceiving others, being wise and not foolish, using time efficiently, not getting drunk, encouraging one another, and submitting to one another.

Ephesians 5:22–27 goes on to describe more specifically this Christlike headship in marriage. Eugene Peterson's contemporary translation of this passage is most communicative:

> *Wives, understand and support your husbands in ways that show your support for Christ. The husband provides leadership to his wife the way Christ does to his church, not by domineering but by cherishing. So just as the church submits to Christ as he exercises such leadership, wives should likewise submit to their husbands.*
>
> *Husbands, go all out in your love for your wives, exactly as Christ did for the church—a love marked by giving, not getting. Christ's love makes the church whole. His words evoke her beauty. Everything he does and says is designed to bring the best out of her, dressing her in dazzling white silk, radiant with holiness. And that is how husbands ought to love their wives* (The Message).

Servant leadership includes the characteristics that Christ modeled:

1. He was clear who He was: Know yourself.
2. He was ready to serve: Serve your wife and family.
3. He did not shy away from the difficult challenges of life (before His crucifixion, Jesus wanted out): Take on life with confidence even when it's tough; hang in there even when you want to bail.
4. He was willing to be vulnerable; He showed compassion, anger, agony—the whole range of emotions: Allow your true feelings to show; open yourself to your wife.
5. He gave up His rights for us: Give up your rights so you can meet her sexual needs.

Relinquish Your Rights

The husband and the wife have the right to have their sexual needs fulfilled with each other in marriage. There is no doubt that God designed and intended sex in marriage, and for that to be a vital ongoing expectation in the marital bond. He designed marriage for sexual fulfillment emotionally, physically, and spiritually.

Your right is sexual fulfillment with your wife; the command is to love your wife as Christ loved the church. Christ's right was to be equal with God; His love for the church gave up that right. Thus, you may have to give up your right for sexual fulfillment with your wife in order to love your wife as Christ loved the church. Again, the apostle Paul provides the teaching:

> *Do nothing from selfishness or empty conceit, but with humility of mind let each of you regard one another as more important than himself; do not merely look out for your own personal interests, but also for the interests of others. Have this attitude in yourselves which was also in Christ Jesus, who, although He existed in the form of God, did not regard equality with God a thing to be grasped, but emptied Himself, taking the form of a bond-servant, and being made in the likeness of men. And being found in appearance as a man, He humbled Himself by becoming obedient to the point of death, even death on a cross* (Phil. 2:3–8 NASB).

According to George Gilder's *Men and Marriage*, "it is men who make the major sacrifice. The man renounces his dream of short-term sexual freedom and self-fulfillment—his male sexuality and self-expression—in order to serve a woman and family for a lifetime. It is a traumatic act of giving up his most profound yearning, his bent for the hunt and the chase, the motorbike and the open road, . . . and immediate excitements. . . . This male sacrifice . . . is essential to civilization" (p. 171). It sounds like a touch of what Christ did for humankind.

Regard the Importance of Your Wife's Needs

If you are to love your wife as Christ loved the church, you are to regard her as more important than you, or her sexual needs more important than yours. That means you have to know her sexual needs. You can know her needs only as she is free and able to tell you her needs. You may say, "But she doesn't have any!" Many people have no need for Christ in their lives. Did that keep Christ from dying for them? No! He gave Himself and accepted them on their terms. He never demands a response to His offer of Himself.

Each person is free to choose Christ's gift of Himself; likewise, your wife needs to be free to choose how she responds to you sexually. That is a tough order, but that is the requirement! She has to be free to let you know where she is and what she desires before she can freely give herself to you. She has to have the freedom to be able to say, "No," before she can say, "Yes."

◆ ◆ ◆

To be free to give herself sexually, your wife must be free to make that choice.

◆ ◆ ◆

On the other hand, you may be the spouse who needs the freedom to say, "No." You may say, "There is no way I can ever keep up with her. She would want sex all the time. I have to make a living and do a few other things in life besides satisfy my wife sexually." All you can do is empty yourself—be available to her and give what you have to give. You are not required to give more than you have. Even Christ did not heal everyone; even He had to get away from the crowds to rest.

Look Out for Her as You Look Out for Yourself

The assumption is that you will look out for your needs; you will accept responsibility for yourself. And that is the way sex works best; each of you is responsible for the pleasure you are able to give and receive in any sexual experience. You are responsible to know yourself and communicate your needs to your wife without demand. This may be difficult to picture.

Look again to the model of Christ. Christ offers Himself. He expresses His passionate desire for all of humankind to accept His offer and invite Him into their lives and become one with Him, but He never pushes Himself on anyone. You may have had Him pushed on you by someone, but that is not how He functions. So with your wife, you express your desires, offer yourself, but allow her total freedom to offer herself to receive the pleasure you have to give her or to enjoy your body for her pleasure.

◆ ◆ ◆

You offer yourself,
but you allow her total freedom to
offer herself to receive your body and
the pleasure you have to give her.

◆ ◆ ◆

The instruction is that you will look out for her interests with the same commitment that you will naturally look out for yourself. When you express your desire for sex and she would rather sit and talk and cuddle, what do you do? The rest of the Ephesians 5 passage as it is expressed in *The Message* may be helpful:

No one abuses his own body, does he? No, he feeds and pampers it. That's how Christ treats us, the church, since we are part of his body. And this is why a man leaves father and mother and cherishes his wife. No longer two, they become "one flesh." This is a huge mystery, and I don't pretend to understand it all. What is clearest to me is the way Christ treats the church. And this provides a good picture of how each husband is to treat his wife, loving himself in loving her, and how each wife is to honor her husband.

As the last chapter suggested, when you go her way, you will bring out the best of her sexuality, and then you will experience deep love. So you talk and cuddle! But you cannot go into the talking and cuddling with the selfish expectation that you will do what she wants to get what you want. It won't work. "Do nothing from selfishness." When you truly lose your life or relinquish your wants, you gain your life or get your deeper needs met. Christ did not empty Himself and die on the cross so that He would be exalted, but that is what happened:

God also has highly exalted Him and given Him the name which is above every name, that at the name of Jesus every knee should bow, of those in heaven, and of those on earth, and of those under the earth" (Phil. 2:9–10).

When you are able to get the focus off what you feel you so desperately need, give yourself to your wife, respect and respond to her desires, affirm and enjoy her to the extent that she is able to give herself to you, sexual fulfillment will result. As you release the fear that your wife will require more of you than you can give or not be what you need her to be sexually, you are more likely to have all the love, passion, and intimacy you deeply desire.

Prepare Yourself for Her

Two family symbolisms used throughout Scripture teach us about our relationship with God. God is represented to us as our Father, and Christ as our Husband, the Bridegroom. They are two very different but equally important symbolisms.

In the case of the sexual relationship in marriage, being Christlike as a husband is being like Christ, the Bridegroom, was with the church, His bride. In the New Testament teaching about Christ coming for His bride (Rev. 21—22), it talks about Him coming in all His glory with armies in white robes. You probably won't approach your wife on a throne adorned and surrounded by armies in white robes, although that could add some humor to a tense situation. Nevertheless, preparing yourself for her will be loving her as Christ loves the church.

Prepare Your Body

During a sexual experience, you and your wife share your bodies most intimately. Coming to sex with a well-groomed body will not only demonstrate your care; it will also invite a positive response.

Not now, Warren. I've got winter breath.

We recommend showering before sex not because we believe the genitals are a dirty part of the body; they are not. Having a clean body means getting rid of body odor and sweat and making sure you smell good and feel nice to be touched anywhere. Showering or bathing together can be a way to connect and feel closer to each other as you begin to share your bodies.

Shaving and brushing your teeth before sex help kissing be more pleasant and passionate. Bad breath is often reported by one spouse as the reason the couple have stopped kissing passionately, yet that spouse may have never told the other that halitosis was the problem. Check that with each other because passionate kissing is a key ingredient to an ongoing vital sex life.

Prepare Your Mind

The mind is often referred to as the primary sexual organ. Your mind controls your body's sexual response, it controls your attitudes about sex, and it controls your sexual feelings.

Your mind-set toward each sexual experience will affect the process and outcome of the interaction. Each time will be different for each of you. You will be coming with different expectations and feelings, depending on various influencing internal and external factors. What happened in the rest of your life the hours before, how you are feeling, what the temperature is, what the room looks like, and many other issues will affect the mental approach toward your time together. That is why it is so important to mesh. Take time to share where each one is mentally and what each would like.

Individual mental preparation even before you connect with each other is a huge asset to sex. Get a sense of what you are bringing to the marital bed and how that will add to or distract from your time with your wife. Picture how you would like to be with her given what you know works best for her and for you. Think through what you know about where she is coming from that day. Picture and plan to love her the way Christ loves the church—give yourself totally on her terms.

Prepare Your Spirit

Having sex is becoming one. That means joining spirits as well as bodies and emotions. Take time to be clear with God and feel replenished spiritually; it will help you be able to give yourself to your wife and to accept and enjoy what she is able to give to you.

The two of you may enhance the depth of your sexual bond by beginning with a spiritual connection. Take time to read the Bible and pray together. Invite God into your sexual experience, and ask Him for all the joy and delight He intends for the two of you as you become one.

Give More

Even though you cannot give for the purpose of getting, giving will most likely be rewarding. Not only can you learn to receive deep pleasure out of the giving itself, but giving to your wife—serving her and caring about her—will likely warm her to want to give herself to you. Just as demand stifles, giving softens.

Demand stifles; giving softens.

Within marriage, each spouse is the other's, but not the other's to possess and control. You are to nurture and cherish each other, and honor, enjoy, and delight in each other's body.

Marriage is a license to freedom without demand;
marriage is not a license to possess and control.

Enjoy your rights and your responsibilities in your sexual relationship with your wife. Learn to freely give her your body without demand for your response or hers. Learn to ravish her body for your pleasure (not for its response) to the extent that she is able to give you that freedom. Learn to love her by serving her, relinquishing your rights, regarding her needs as you do your own, and preparing yourself for your sexual times together. As you give without expectation, you will get.

> *I am my beloved's,*
> *And his desire is for me.*
> *Come, my beloved, let us go out into the country,*

Let us spend the night in the villages.
Let us rise early and go to the vineyards;
Let us see whether the vine has budded
And its blossoms have opened,
And whether the pomegranates have bloomed.
There I will give you my love
(Song 7:10–12 NASB).

Chapter 5

Sex Is Not a Spectator Sport

"It's no fun! Hers don't work! There is no response! All I can say is, what a shame! It's a waste!" exclaimed Mark. He was frustrated with his wife's beautiful body because she did not get aroused easily or regularly when he stimulated her genitals. He had difficulty enjoying intimacy with her; he watched for the response he could produce.

Watching for the result rather than focusing on the enjoyment of each other's body and the pleasure of being together will interfere with attaining the result.

◆ ◆ ◆

Watching is demanding;
demands inhibit.

◆ ◆ ◆

When you watch the Red Sox play, you enjoy yourself. Your body and emotions react to the ups and downs of the game. Watching Michael Jordan dunk one for the Chicago Bulls while he is suspended in air is thrilling whether or not you're a fan. When Orel Hershiser was pitching one shutout after another, you could get vicarious elation from his success.

There is no pressure on you to perform when you are watching someone else at play. However, if the player starts watching himself, his performance is likely to spiral downward. That is what *The Inner Game of Tennis* by Timothy Gallwey is all about. The book helps the tennis player improve his game by using his anxiety about performance as positive energy and power behind his moves. It helps him keep his focus on the game and on his actions instead of watching while he is playing.

Sex works the same way. If you are a player in sex, watching interferes with your and/or your wife's responses rather than heightening them. If you are watching someone else play at sex, as in the movies or pornography, your body will respond. When you are mentally outside the event looking in at yourself or your wife as you play in the game of sex, you will lose. William Masters and Virginia Johnson first described this concept of spectatoring in *Human Sexual Inadequacy*:

> Through their fears of performance (the fear of failing sexually), their emotional and mental involvement in the sexual activity they share with their partner is essentially nonexistent. The thought . . . and the action are totally dissociated by reason of the individual's involuntary assumption of a spectator's role during active sexual participation (p. 11).

――――――― ◆ ◆ ◆ ―――――――

Spectatoring:
When you are mentally outside looking in
as you play in the game of sex, you will lose.

――――――― ◆ ◆ ◆ ―――――――

YOU WATCHING YOU

You come home from work. It's Friday evening. You've had a long week. You feel the tension between your wife and the kids when you walk in. The baby-sitter will be there soon so you and your wife can go out to dinner, come home, and slip into the back bedroom without the kids knowing. Sex hasn't been working too well for you lately; you get into it and then you lose your responsiveness. You start having mixed feelings between positive anticipation of being together and concern about your performance.

You have started spectatoring. Without understanding how your performance anxiety is interfering, you have moved outside the experience, started watching your body's response, and hurt yourself and your time with your wife. The secret to counter spectatoring is to remove all demands for response and focus on the enjoyment of your bodies—the pleasure of being together.

———— ◆ ◆ ◆ ————

The secret to stop spectatoring:
Remove all demands for response and
focus on the enjoyment of your bodies.

———— ◆ ◆ ◆ ————

Response is not nearly as important as the fun you and your wife can have and the love you feel when you are together. But it will be hard to convince yourself of that. Once the spectatoring has become a habit, it has the effect of keeping control on what you think and feel. It interrupts the natural flow. You start placing demands on yourself to get your body to work. The more you feel the pressure and concern, the less your body is likely to work. It is a vicious circle.

For sex to work, you need emotional abandonment. You cannot think about how your body is responding. Anytime you try to force your body to do something it can do only without demand, you will keep it from doing the very thing you want it to do. Usually during sex, the good feelings of being together, of caressing your wife's body and her caressing yours, and of sexual excitement will engage you. That is, until—for whatever reason—your body does not respond the way you expect it to.

———— ◆ ◆ ◆ ————

Emotional abandonment is necessary
for sex to work.

———— ◆ ◆ ◆ ————

Sometimes your body may not respond the way you expect it to because either you or your wife has unrealistic sexual expectations. For example, a couple may seek help from us, and the woman complains of the man's lack of ejaculatory control. As we take the history and evaluate their problem, we discover that she expects him to be able to thrust vigorously for twenty minutes without stopping or ejaculating. Neither of them knew that would be difficult or impossible for most men, so he became more and more anxious about his inability to please his wife and she became more unhappy with his "lack of control."

Other times a woman expects that her forty- or fifty-year-old husband will be able to have intercourse, ejaculate, and be restimulated to another erection without a rest period. Most men require anywhere from twenty minutes to twenty hours to be restimulated to another erection after an ejaculation.

Still other times the man complains that he lacks sexual desire. Then we discover that he expects to come to the sexual experience already erect, and he equates arousal with desire instead of accepting the fact that desire usually precedes arousal. So your body may not be the problem; misinformation about what is normal may put unrealistic pressure on you to perform.

◆ ◆ ◆

Remove all unrealistic expectations to perform by making sure you have accurate information.

◆ ◆ ◆

For many other reasons, spectatoring can invade your sexual relationship and cause performance anxiety. Fatigue, illness, stress, distraction, guilt, a critical wife, anxiety, depression, and medication are all factors that can interfere with your body's natural response and start you watching yourself.

◆ ◆ ◆

Remove circumstances that interfere with your body's natural response.

◆ ◆ ◆

Whatever the reason for its beginning, you can break spectatoring by removing all demands for your response and focusing on pleasure. To become an active player and stop watching yourself, try taking these steps:

1. Rule out intercourse. Sex does not equal intercourse. We confirm Dr. Warwick Williams's emphasis that "lovemaking means literally that—interacting physically and emotionally. . . . Arousal, intercourse, and orgasm or ejaculation are nonessential, and simply possible lovemaking options" (*Rekindling Desire*, p. 109).

Stopping short of intercourse or orgasm—not in a punitive, withholding manner, but out of personal restraint—can teach you to savor the wonderful sensations of the moment. It can create the added dimension of desire for each other that you may long for. A man typically goes for more when less keeps both of you hungry for more.

◆ ◆ ◆

Go for less, not more;
it will reduce demand and
keep you both hungry for more.

◆ ◆ ◆

2. Redefine good sex. Good sex does not depend on the involuntary responses of your body that you cannot control. Bernie Zilbergeld, Ph.D., said it well in *The New Male Sexuality*: "You're having good sex if you feel good about yourself, and good about your partner, and good about what you are doing. And later you have a good time of reflection" (p. 67).

3. Accept sexual anxiety as normal. Men will be anxious about sex sometime during their marriage. Young, newly married men will be anxious about their experience. Many men are anxious about penis size. Other men are anxious about satisfying their wives. Middle-aged and older men become anxious about the changes in their sexual response as the result of aging. They may worry about erections and ejaculation.

When you can accept anxiety as normal, you can make it work for you rather than against you. You can turn it into positive energy.

4. Define your conditions for sex. You may need to be free of anxiety to be able to engage in any sexual contact with your wife. That is fine. You may need to feel rested and free of stress or safe and positively connected with your wife. Certainly, you need to know that the sexual time will be free of demands and unrealistic expectations.

5. Distract from evaluating bodily responses. The best distraction is to get lost in each other. Talking to each other about your enjoyment of the other's body is a great affirmation and distraction.

6. Focus on pleasing sensations. Soak in the touch both as you are caressing and as you are being caressed. Enjoy her body for your pleasure; allow her to enjoy yours for her pleasure. Experiment with a variety of sensations. Choose different textured objects to pleasure. Use other parts of your bodies to caress. Use your penis like a paintbrush to bring pleasure to her genitals without entry.

7. Verbalize anxiety and feelings of demand and spectatoring. The most effective way to diffuse the power of negative thoughts is to say them when you note them. For example, you and your wife are back in the bedroom starting to get ready for sexual contact, and you think, *What if I lose it tonight?* Tell her immediately. Simply verbalizing shifts the thought from the right side of the brain where it controls you to the left, or verbal, side, releasing the control it has on your body.

8. Picture positive sexual feelings, actions, and responses. Do not allow negative pictures. The more you rehearse the positive and eliminate the negative, the more quickly your experiences will be free of the negative and filled with warm, loving passion.

WATCHING HER

Have you ever watched a hovering boss or a hovering mother? Every move the employee or the child makes is met with an evaluation or a question: "Oh, you are going to put it in that account?"; "Don't you think it would work better if you started with this problem?"; "I noticed that you didn't get finished with your project yesterday"; "You would do better if you did it this way."

Some men are hovering lovers. The more the husband hovers, the less the wife is able to experience her sexuality. She becomes discouraged with her lack of sexual vibrancy. She feels diminishing interest in sex, and she has fewer and less intense sexual responses. He sees her as a problem to fix, so he makes more and more "loving" suggestions about what she might do to help her response. He is watching her, and now she is watching herself.

Carol and Allen had completed the sexual therapy process to treat what they had defined as her lack of sexual desire and decreased sexual arousal and release. We had defined the problem as his watching her and had helped him look at why her sexuality was so important to his emotional security—an issue we will address more thoroughly in the next chapter. In the process of sexual therapy, they had retrained themselves to get the focus off her sexuality and onto the pleasure of being together. They were having good sexual times. And not at all surprising to us, she was responding sexually, not every time, but certainly more often than when they first sought help.

Last week Carol called for help. They were both discouraged. She had not been "in the mood" for several weeks. With his encouragement she had put on a sexy outfit to see if that would help, but that didn't really do it for her as it had the last time she tried that. They went ahead anyway "hoping the feelings would follow the actions" as we "had taught them." She did get in the mood for a little bit, but then he had to get up and close the shades and that stopped her "mood" completely. Then the next time they were together and having intercourse, he stopped thrusting and nicely suggested that if she would move, that would probably help her "get into it." He then made the comment, "You're not trying." She got furious.

She reported to us that she was feeling stubborn. She found herself not wanting to do any of the things she knew would help. What she hadn't seen was that her old resistance had been rekindled in response to his ongoing evaluation of her body's response. She was trying to force her body to respond in ways that it could respond only without demand or without being watched. Fortunately, identifying the principles they had learned and their slip back into their old habits brought laughter and the ability to reaffirm and reapply what they had learned would work.

————— ◆ ◆ ◆ —————

A woman cannot force her body to respond;
it can respond only without demand or
without being watched.

————— ◆ ◆ ◆ —————

Like Allen who was watching Carol or Mark who was upset because his wife's genitals didn't respond to his stimulation, your hovering *must* stop if you are watching your wife and evaluating her sexuality in any way! If your ability to enjoy yourself during sex depends on her body's involuntary sexual responses, her body will never respond. Your monitoring her will interfere.

————— ◆ ◆ ◆ —————

Your monitoring her will
inevitably interfere with her
body's natural responses.

————— ◆ ◆ ◆ —————

The more a husband watches his wife's sexual interest, arousal, and response, the greater demand she will experience. Her need to feel desire, excitement, and response to his stimulation will make it less likely that any of these natural sexual responses will occur. Knowing this is the first step in stopping your hovering, but this knowledge alone will not necessarily stop your hovering and evaluating.

You can make some tangible efforts to distract you from watching her:

1. **Be deliberate in your affirmation of her.** Get active in focusing on what you enjoy about her body—how it feels, how it looks, how good it feels when it touches you and you touch it. Do not focus on how it responds or moves or does anything; just focus on what is. Express your enjoyment of her.

2. **Distract yourself from watching her.** If watching is a habit for you, it will automatically creep into your sexual life. You will have to take control of that tendency by learning to recognize it, stopping it, and distracting yourself by putting your focus elsewhere.

3. **Focus on the sensations of touch.** Enjoy her body for you. Learn to know it. Explore every skin surface, her hair, her face, feet, hands, and every crevice. Wherever she is touching you, soak in the touch. In a positive selfish way, get the focus off her and onto how wonderful it feels to be touched.

4. **Allow her to listen to her body's hunger for touch and go after what she needs.** Respond to her invitations and requests without hesitation or direction or correction. Let her lead.

5. **Agree to enjoy the other's body freely.** Take responsibility to let the other know if the other's enjoyment of your body becomes negative. Then redirect and invite what would feel positive.

KEEPING SCORE

It was February of 1977. A couple asked us for help concerning the husband's erections. They had been married twenty years and had a wonderful sex life until October 1976. If you remember, 1976 was the bicentennial year. The couple decided that they would have sex two hundred times during 1976 as their private contribution to the Bicentennial. This is a true story! October arrived, and they realized they had had sex only 85 times; they had 115 times left to carry out in only three months. Keeping score became a pressure; it was no longer a fun project.

Sex is for pleasure and for procreation. Whenever sex becomes goal oriented, the body's responses will be affected, and enjoyment will be stifled.

◆ ◆ ◆

*Whenever sex becomes goal oriented,
the body's responses will be affected,
and enjoyment will be stifled.*

◆ ◆ ◆

Counting sexual experiences or responses may happen as a result of an anxious, sexually demanding man (or woman), infertility struggles, clearing the sperm from the system after a vasectomy (a procedure done to keep a man from being able to impregnate a woman), or setting a goal for any reason, such as the couple's Bicentennial effort. Once you start monitoring and keeping score, the focus is off the process and on the goal. The efforts to reach that goal will be sexually destructive.

The November before our last child was born in December (also 1976!), we decided that Cliff would have a vasectomy after he became clear that he would not want to father more children, even if something happened to me and the children. However, we had not decided who would take the responsibility for our family planning decision until we went to the birthing preparation classes and he felt too old to be there. The closeness between his vasectomy and the delivery of Kristine left little time and energy for Cliff to have enough ejaculations to meet his doctor's quota to ensure that the sperm were out of the system by the time we were ready to resume our sexual life. So we started counting ejaculations. You can guess what happened!

You may have started counting. When was the last time you had sex? The time before that? How long did you last? Did she have an orgasm? How many orgasms did she have? When was the last time she initiated? How many times have you initiated? How many times did she kiss you passionately in the last week? Whatever you are counting, that very activity or response will die. You can take charge of your sexual experience and make these things happen, but you cannot stand back and keep score. Sex is not a spectator sport.

QUESTIONING

Questioning is a form of hovering, watching, and comparing: "Was that good for you, honey?" or "Are you feeling anything?" or "Are you in the mood?" or "What about tonight?" or "Would you like to?"

——————— ◆ ◆ ◆ ———————

Sex is not a spectator sport;
sex happens best
when you don't keep score.

——————— ◆ ◆ ◆ ———————

Each question represents some expectation without taking personal responsibility to express what you want. A man asks questions because he is asking how well he is doing. The questions reflect the sense of sex as a competition. Indirectly, the man is asking, "How many points did I get on this one?" or "Did I measure up?" The competition may be against some real or imaginary lover, some standard, or the woman herself. Interrogation intrudes and provokes defensiveness rather than accepts, enjoys, and shares yourself.

Initiating

In the decision to have sex, share what you would like and respect her response to that. Don't ask what she would like. Follow her lead by offering yourself but letting her respond to your offer and/or offer herself. Avoid questions and demands when initiating.

A Put-Off:	*A Lure:*
"Would you give me a kiss?"	Just kiss her; start gently.
"What about tonight?"	"I'd like to play tonight."
"Are you in the mood?"	"Boy, am I in the mood!"

Experiencing

This may sound like a broken record, but we'll say it again: Get into sex for your pleasure. Enjoy her body; share your body. Allow her to do the same, and do not attend to or question how that is going for her. Your sensitivity is important; keep the sensitivity responding to her lead rather than evaluating how it is going.

Ineffective:	*Effective:*
"Does this feel good?"	"Yum, does this feel good!"
"Are you feeling anything?"	"I could do this forever."
"Am I in the right spot?"	"That is the most wonderful spot."

Affirming

Affirm rather than evaluate your sexual experiences. Express your enjoyment and delight. Avoid questions. Questions tend to imply demand. Being sexual therapists and hearing couples talk about their sex lives all day, we sometimes have fun using evaluation as affirmation. We might say, "Now, that was a ten!" Statements of positive evaluation can be affirming if used carefully.

Demanding:	*Enjoying:*
"Was that good for you?"	"I sure enjoyed you."
"Did you have an orgasm?"	"That was an explosive one for me. Hope I didn't leave you behind."
"Did I do better that time?"	"I felt more comfortable that time."

Interrogation—question asking—is a way of protecting your feelings of vulnerability. It keeps you out of the spotlight and puts the spotlight on her. It is distancing. It elicits performance anxiety and is a form of spectatoring. In business, interrogation may be the tool to obtain needed information quickly. In bed, questions put you on her side of the bed without being invited and push her right out of bed.

Since sex is not a spectator sport, the sooner you can catch and change any spectatoring habits such as watching yourself, watching your wife, keeping score, or questioning, the freer you will find sex to be. Rid yourself of these cumbersome habits. Take the risk; be a player. Jump into the game with all of your being. Sure, you could get hurt, but you also could stir up a lot of ecstasy. And that would be well worth the risk.

A woman of gentle grace gets respect,
  but men of rough violence grab for loot
(Prov. 11:16, *The Message*).

Chapter 6

Sex: A Path to Intimacy

As sexual therapists and seminar leaders, we have talked to thousands of couples about the pains and the joys they have experienced sexually. We find that sexual needs are changing. Fewer couples are seeking help for technical sexual dysfunction, such as impotence, premature ejaculation, and orgasmic inhibition. With many self-help books, for example, our *Restoring the Pleasure*, available to couples, they are dealing with these issues in the privacy of the bedroom. However, couples are desperately seeking help to overcome the intimacy barriers in their sexual relationships.

As couples learn to talk and listen to each other effectively, as they learn to give and receive physical pleasure, and as they learn about each other as sexual persons—male and female—barriers are broken down, differences are accepted, demands are relieved, and newer levels of love, passion, and intimacy are discovered.

WHEN HER SEXUALITY = YOUR MALENESS

A man's sexual intimacy may be interrupted because his maleness depends on the sexuality of his wife. Since a woman is changeable, unpredictable, and wavelike in her sexuality, relying on your wife's desire for you and responsiveness to you will not be great for building the security that allows true intimacy to grow in your relationship.

> **Myth:** *A real man is married to a woman who wants him sexually, loves his body, and responds to his touch with erotic ecstasy.*

When your self-worth depends on your ability to sexually fulfill your wife, both of you will become pressured to achieve that goal. Even though a woman's sexual responsiveness and enjoyment are naturally fulfilling to a man, a focus on producing her responsiveness to validate you will take away from her sexual enjoyment, make her responsiveness less likely, and decrease your pleasure. Love, passion, and intimacy will be destroyed.

――――― ◆ ◆ ◆ ―――――

Sex will not be great when your self-worth depends on your
wife's sexual responsiveness;
love, passion, and intimacy will be destroyed.

――――― ◆ ◆ ◆ ―――――

Go for Less, Not More

Men are raised to score. The faster they score and the more they score, the better they are. Yet we have been saying sex is not about scoring. That is because women are quite the opposite. When men score with women, women feel like objects. A woman needs to feel loved and supported; a woman needs to know that her husband values her as a person apart from sex. When she feels valued, she is eager to open herself up to him sexually.

A woman's sexual enthusiasm can be destroyed by her husband's sexual eagerness, especially when his eagerness is connected with insecurity or the need to prove himself through her sexual responsiveness. That is the reason for our "lag behind" rule for men. If a man always keeps his sexual intensity and activity just less than hers, he will keep her hungry for more.

――――― ◆ ◆ ◆ ―――――

A woman will stay hungry for sex
when her husband lags behind her
in sexual intensity and activity.

――――― ◆ ◆ ◆ ―――――

Sexual anorexia in a woman is often a response to having been force-fed sexually by an overeager husband. It reminds us of setting out food for young children. If you don't give them very much, they cry for more. If you overload their plates, they play with their food and seem disinterested in eating.

───── ◆ ◆ ◆ ─────

Sexual force-feeding leads to female sexual anorexia.

───── ◆ ◆ ◆ ─────

Keep your wife hungry, but not starving. Enjoy every inch of her body before you go near the hot spots. Stroke her slowly everywhere and do it for your enjoyment, not for the response your touching produces. Let her invite more direct stimulation. Don't resist when she invites. That can be frustrating and make her angry. Respond to her invitation with delight. What if she never feels secure enough to invite? Work out a deal so that you can know when she is ready for more. Err on the side of enjoying too long rather than pursuing too soon.

───── ◆ ◆ ◆ ─────

Err on the side of enjoying too long rather than pursuing too soon.

───── ◆ ◆ ◆ ─────

If your natural instincts get you carried away and you revert to pursuing too fast and too intensely, back off as soon as you notice her tighten up. We have a fun game that we enjoy when Cliff's aggression is too intense for Joyce. Cliff will play hard to get: "Oh, no, I'm really too tired tonight"; "That's way too intense for me; can we slow down?"; "Do we have to?" It is an instant cure. It adds fun and triggers Joyce's ardor.

Remember Her Needs

A woman gets frustrated with a man because he doesn't remember. A source of much contempt from a wife to her husband can be that she is convinced she has told him many times exactly what she likes sexually, but he does not do what she asked. Yet he protests that he does not know what she wants or asks why she doesn't respond to what he does. What happens? We have often said that a man's memory is in inverse proportion to his arousal. A friend suggested that his blood is no longer in his brain. With arousal, the blood leaves his brain and goes where there is no memory!

There are two clear reasons why wives believe their husbands should know what they like and why husbands seem not to know. First, husbands seem to have difficulty really believing and remembering that wives like sex so differently from what is natural for them. Second, wives seem to have a tough time taking ongoing responsibility for keeping their husbands informed of their sexual desires and needs. At some primitive level both men and women believe men are the sexual experts. A wife will continue to fantasize that if her husband truly loves her, he will sweep her off her feet sexually. He will be the knight in shining armor who turns on her ravishing hunger for him. When that does not happen, she is disappointed that she has to tell him what she does and does not like.

———— ◆◆◆ ————

Both men and women falsely believe that the man is the sexual expert who will make his wife ravishingly hungry for him.

———— ◆◆◆ ————

Both of you can accept responsibility to reverse your natural inclinations: You recognize that what is natural for you may not be natural for her; she realizes that there is no way for you to know her whim in any given moment. As you become responsible to listen to and go with her and she listens to and communicates her needs and desires, you will remember and she will be happy, and intimacy will evolve.

WHEN SEX IS MORE THAN SEX

The majority of the spouses we see in sexual therapy today long to be loved intimately and validated by each other. They struggle with relationship discord, shame and control issues, anger, abuse, and fears of abandonment that keep them from knowing each other intimately. And that lack of or difficulty with intimacy affects their sexual lives.

According to David M. Schnarch, the author of *Constructing the Sexual Crucible* and the leading proponent of finding sexual fulfillment through sexual intimacy, "People have boring, monotonous sex because intense sex and intimacy are far more threatening and scary than they can imagine, and require more adult autonomy and ego strength than they can muster" (from "Inside the Sexual Crucible" in *Networker*, March/April 1993, p. 43).

When inner strength and autonomy are not there for one or both spouses, the relationship is negatively affected in ways that infiltrate their sexual life. As partners learn about each other and learn to give and receive pleasure without demand, healing takes place, and intimacy builds.

Destructive Relationship Patterns

When Your Need for Validation Spells S-E-X

For many men, sex releases the tension in their bodies and is the avenue for feeling good about themselves and being more open and vulnerable to experience love with their wives. The man who needs sex for his validation, however, is an extreme of that natural tendency.

If you need sex for validation, you have come to marriage lacking some confidence in relation to women, particularly sexually. You may not have had a rich dating history. You may be sensitive to rejection because of your history with women, not getting unconditional love from your mother, or your lack of a strong connection with your father.

Your wife describes you as a wonderful, warm, caring, involved husband and father. You probably saved sex for marriage and now are disappointed because of what both you and your wife define as her lack of sexual desire.

Because of your sensitivity to rejection, she can never want you enough to fill that void inside you. The way you experience the difficulty, however, is that before marriage she was eager and alive and now she "doesn't desire you."

Early in your marriage, maybe on your honeymoon, she wasn't as interested or as responsive as she had been or you imagined she would be. She may have brought some sexual hesitancies to your marriage. Her not being as available as you needed her to be triggered your deep insecurity. She sensed your negative reaction to her natural waves of sexual interest and intensity, so she either had sex to make you happy or withdrew even more because of the demand your response communicated. Whether she went with pleasing you or withdrawing completely, her sexuality was invalidated. Sex was taken away from her; it changed from something expectant that she desired to something you needed from her.

The more she felt your need to have sex to make you feel good, the more she resisted your neediness or performed out of duty, and the less satisfying sex became for both of you. What you really needed was for her to need you and desire you passionately. The very thing you needed and knew you deserved was zapped away because of your desperate need to be needed.

————— ◆ ◆ ◆ —————

The more you need her to need you,
the more her need for you will be zapped away
because you so desperately need to be needed.

————— ◆ ◆ ◆ —————

Your anxiousness about her lack of desire led you to urgently seek to correct her problem. She became more and more discouraged about herself sexually. The more you sought a solution for her and not yourself, the more she felt your push and demand for sex rather than affirmation, connection, and invitation of her as a person.

This destructive relationship pattern caused sex to be more than sex. It probably continued until you got professional help, separated, or resolved to focus on the other positive elements of your marriage and family. You may have resigned yourself to the fact that sex would be less than you hoped for, and she accepted that she was not very sexual. What a sad confusion of reality!

Fortunately, you have the solution to this destructive relationship pattern inside you. The solution is twofold: (1) You separate your need for validation from your wife's sexuality, and (2) you affirm any little evidence of her sexuality. Her sexuality will resurface and will indeed validate you. Sounds simple? It isn't. But you can do it! You may need the support of a professional therapist to see how you are continuing to make your wife responsible to personally validate you through sex.

————— ◆ ◆ ◆ —————

As you separate your need for
validation from your wife's sexuality
and validate her,
her sexuality will resurface, and
you will be validated.

————— ◆ ◆ ◆ —————

Your goal is to eliminate your need to be validated by sex. To do this, you need to rule out ejaculation and intercourse with your wife and just enjoy sexual pleasure and intimacy with her. The most difficult requirement of this learning process is that you take care of your sexual release needs through self-stimulation. During self-stimulation, picture enjoying your wife's body for your pleasure without attending in your mind to her response. The purpose of the self-stimulation is to separate sexual release with your wife from your need for personal validation.

Once you have accomplished the goal, you will be able to enjoy a full, free, nondemanding sexual relationship with your wife. God's plan for you in your marriage is not self-stimulation. It is to experience the rewards of true intimacy with your wife. However, God's ideal for you can be achieved only as you are willing to suffer the tearing pain you will experience in separating your sexual response with her from your need for validation. Then you will be able to freely fulfill the command of 1 Corinthians 7 that teaches that each spouse's body is the other's and that you are to mutually and freely enjoy each other.

A critical component for both you and your wife to reestablish your sexual freedom with each other will be to start over in learning to give and receive pleasure without the demand for her to validate you with her interest or responsiveness. Learning to delight in each other once again will usually require ruling out past sexual behaviors and starting over using a step-by-step process of taking turns touching and receiving touch. Start with a foot and hand caress. Move to caressing each other's faces, then backs, then total bodies except for breasts and genitals. When you are able to give and receive pleasure freely without demand, genitals can be included. Stop and talk whenever either of you experiences old feelings or pressures. You will learn to give your bodies to each other for pleasure only, without the pressure for her responsiveness to validate your maleness.

When Your Performance Is Necessary to Validate Her

Women sometimes have a similar need to be personally validated through sex. Your wife may feel you don't care about her enough to delay your ejaculation unrealistically, get an erection without any stimulation, be restimulated after ejaculation, or enable her to have an orgasm during intercourse. She needs you to sexually respond on her terms by demand in order to feel loved.

———— ◆ ◆ ◆ ————

A wife who needs to be validated
through sex will need you to
respond on her terms by demand
in order to feel loved.

———— ◆ ◆ ◆ ————

Your wife was probably hurt by men during her childhood. She is look-ing for proof that you won't hurt her. Out of her inability to trust that you can be there for her, she sets the conditions so there is almost no way for you to meet her requirements.

The skills of a professional would help her and take the pressure off you. Your strength can also help. Be consistent in separating what you can do for her and what you can't. For example, you can reassure with words and actions that you love her, you will be there for her, and you will not violate her. However, be clear with her that you will not be able to regain your erection after ejaculation because that is physically impossible. It will help to let her know that your inability to get an erection after ejaculation may seem that you don't care, and that is understandable, given her history. But she needs to understand that your physical inability to meet her perfor-mance demands has absolutely nothing to do with your care for her.

———— ◆ ◆ ◆ ————

Separate what you can do for your wife
from what you cannot;
affirm your love
without conforming to her performance demands.

———— ◆ ◆ ◆ ————

When Anger Interrupts Intimacy

If intimacy is frightening, anger may be safer. You may be reluctant to accept that you may choose anger over intimacy, but at least consider the possibility.

◆ ◆ ◆

If intimacy is frightening, anger may be safer.

◆ ◆ ◆

Anger can be a personal issue. Your personal anger can create intense sexual demand in marriage. One man constantly belittled and distrusted his wife's sexuality because his mother had violated his father by having an affair. As a young boy, he had become his father's confidant and helper in catching his mother in action. Another man left therapy because he could not see his part in his wife's suppressed sexuality. He was angry with his mother for how she treated his father. She frequently pushed his father away. Other men have anger because of physical abuse or emotional neglect from the father. Whatever the source, the old anger is brought into the sexual relationship and used either passively or actively to destroy intimacy.

Anger can also be triggered in the relationship. Paul and Patricia had been married only six months when they called for our help with their sexual relationship. Neither of them had a positive word to say about the other. They expressed contempt, criticism, defensiveness, and stonewalling—all of the four risk factors that Dr. John Gottman's research identified as "the four horsemen" that invade relationships that fail in *Why Marriages Succeed or Fail.*

Attempting to focus on their sexual relationship felt like treating a cut on the hand when the person is going into heart failure. But sex was what they saw as the problem. After feedback about what we saw as the issues, we started giving sexual retraining assignments. The first week ended that process. The four horsemen trampled right through all the assignments. They completed none as directed. Anger completely interrupted their sex life.

He was passive in the expression of his anger; she was aggressive. She pursued; he resisted. She got angrier and angrier as he failed to meet her expectations in sharing household responsibilities and relationship accountability. He became more and more passive as he felt controlled and pursued. She blamed his avoidance on his problem with intimacy; he blamed her for not allowing him any peace.

Patricia needed to get out of the pursuing, critical role before it was possible to deal with his resistance. Both participated in the avoidance of intimacy—she actively sought connection in ways that pushed him farther away, and he was overwhelmed by her intensity and persistence.

Anger can be more subtle. For some couples, it shows up only in sex. She resists sex because he pushes her to have sex. He is upset and complains because she resists. She needs to be validated; he needs to be desired. He approaches the way he would like to be approached. He does not understand that the best way to approach her is to connect with her emotionally and validate her as a person. His expression of sexual need makes her angry. Her lack of need makes him angry. As both partners are able to understand how their anger is sabotaging and make their differences work for them by reversing their destructive pattern, anger dissipates and intimacy builds.

We had the rewarding experience of working with a couple with this pattern. After thirty years of hurt because of his expressing anger through pushing and her expressing anger by resisting, they were ready to dissolve their marriage. We were their last-ditch effort.

The barriers between them softened after the initial assessment and feedback sessions. In the process of gathering data, we discovered that each had been sexually abused as a child. Neither knew of the hurt the other brought into the sex life. With their permission, we shared that information in the feedback session. Sharing those hurts brought a caring response from each to the other. That was the beginning of their building a mutually satisfying sexual relationship. The sexual retraining process moved quickly and successfully from that first day on. The walls were down. All they needed were the steps to learn to share positive sexual experiences for the first time in thirty years.

When Control Issues Keep Sex Safe

Control may be even safer than anger in protecting you from fear of intimacy with your wife. When she wants you sexually, you find it difficult to respond (always, of course, with a valid reason), but you complain because you and she are not having sex as often as you would like.

◆ ◆ ◆

*Control may be even safer than anger
in protecting you from your fear of intimacy.*

◆ ◆ ◆

There are other ways control may prevent sexual intimacy. Maybe your wife does not want sex with you because you ejaculate prematurely, but she refuses to do the exercises with you in order for you to learn ejaculatory control. That is an effective way to protect her from the vulnerability of intimacy.

Control issues often surface in our practice as resistance to sexual retraining. The couple or individual comes to resolve a sexual problem but then sabotages the success of the process by not working the program. The stated reasons are lack of discipline, not enough time, they don't think it will work, they already know, he/she never initiates, or other similar excuses.

Schnarch reported in *Constructing the Sexual Crucible* that he found that when sexual therapy failed, the difficulty was a lack of capacity for intimacy. You may be hesitant to be totally yourself in the presence of your wife. Maybe being yourself was not safe in your childhood family, and now it is virtually impossible to be that open and vulnerable during sex. Your wife may participate in your difficulty. She may be critical or have anger issues or lack unconditional love for you. You long for closeness, but you cannot risk letting it happen. So you seek help but then find reasons not to complete the process. Then you carry around inside a high degree of loneliness anxiety. The steps toward intimacy need to be small enough and in your control so that you can risk in tiny increments.

Personal Issues

Shame

Shame interferes with sex in marriage. When sex is associated with shame, sex is passionate when it occurs outside marriage or is connected with shame-producing fantasies or actions.

— ◆ ◆ ◆ —

Shame interferes with sex in marriage but heightens passion outside marriage.

— ◆ ◆ ◆ —

As one woman expressed it, "I was so sexual before marriage that we had intense struggles keeping from having intercourse. I shut down when I was standing at the altar saying my vows. The thought hit me: *I can't imag-*

ine others knowing that now that we are married we will be having sex." And years later they still had not had sex. She involuntarily closed up the muscle that controls the opening of the vagina, and he was not able to penetrate her. Her shame began with becoming sexually responsive to her father's pornography as a young girl.

Shame associated with sex may have begun with pornography or with other premature or inappropriate sexual exposure. It could have been overt or subtle. It could have happened when as a child there were inappropriate boundaries in the home: a young boy slept with his mother or older sister, a father masturbated in the same room with his daughter while occupying separate beds, a child slept in the same room while the parents carried on their sexual relationship, an adolescent daughter was nude with her father, or the child's innocence and sexual development were not protected.

Shame is a heavy burden to carry. Breaking the connection between sex and shame takes deliberate work and positive step-by-step building of sex in marriage. That effort will bring greater joy and freedom to your sex life.

Abandonment

When abandonment occurred during the first year of life, the capacity for sexual intimacy will have to be learned in marriage. Abandonment could have been physical or emotional. You may have been adopted and not bonded with your adoptive mother and father until after age one. Your mother or primary caregiver may have been hospitalized and taken away from you during that first year. Your mother may have been emotionally absent because of depression or grief in response to a death in the family or inability to be close and warm.

You may have lost a parent before age thirteen or fourteen. The death of a parent, especially the opposite-sex parent, may have left you with extreme difficulty allowing sexual intimacy with your spouse. One man whose mother died of diabetes during his preschool years would fall asleep or lose his erection when he got involved sexually with his wife.

The path to intimacy from abandonment is a tough climb up a steep mountain. Intimacy is the opposite of abandonment. The fear of intimacy is the fear of abandonment. Trust must be built with a secure giving spouse who is uncommonly consistent and emotionally available.

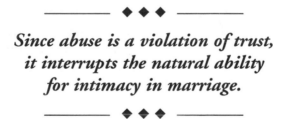

Intimacy is the opposite of abandonment. The fear of intimacy is the fear of abandonment.

Abuse

Whether the abuse was physical, emotional, or sexual, you learned that being close is not safe. Thus, being sexually intimate in marriage becomes exceedingly difficult. Safety is the essential ingredient for allowing yourself to be totally you in the presence of another. You may be able to have intercourse, but the idea of pleasuring and sharing deeply of your inner worlds, emotionally and sexually, will take willingness to risk and careful training.

Since abuse is a violation of trust, it interrupts the natural ability for intimacy in marriage.

Victims of sexual abuse describe a distinct pattern. As children, they either withdrew and felt shame or were aggressive and angry. They felt different from other children. They report having had heightened sexual awareness as children, they have a tendency to be sexually promiscuous or at least highly interested outside marriage, and they shut down sexually as they approached marriage or soon after marriage.

Overcoming abuse and bonding intimately in marriage is a very rewarding process. You finally can get the love you desperately want. However, you need to work through the pain of the abuse. You can do that by talking with a therapist or a group of other victims of abuse or by working through self-help resources with a supportive spouse or friend. You will carry scars into your sexual relationship with your spouse; nevertheless, deep and intimate sexual fulfillment is definitely attainable.

Poor Self-Esteem

Poor self-esteem can come from many sources. For whatever reason, you did not experience the personal validation you needed to believe in yourself. For example, you may not feel comfortable with your body. You may be attractive by all external standards, but you see only flaws in yourself. Your negative feelings about yourself may make it difficult for you to take responsibility for sex and may keep you from sexually validating your wife.

———— ◆ ◆ ◆ ————

Not feeling good about yourself or your body may make it difficult for you to take responsibility for sex and to sexually validate your wife.

———— ◆ ◆ ◆ ————

Self-esteem and body image can mature in a loving, committed marriage with a wife who adores you. Being touched in nondemand ways can help you feel accepted and help you accept yourself and your body. You can take action to improve aspects of your body or yourself that would increase your personal positive regard. You might also acquire increased self-worth through achieving external accomplishments or through becoming a positive parent.

As you gain positive regard for yourself, you will be empowered to take responsibility more fully for your sexual relationship and to respect the sexuality of your wife. As that happens, you will no longer need sex for validation. Instead, sex will be an expression of your good feelings about yourself and your wife and will become an expression of true intimacy.

Addiction

Sexual addictions counteract sexual intimacy. In an addiction, the stimulus for arousal and release is outside the person and usually outside an intimate relationship. Rather than losing himself with his wife, the man sells himself to pornographic magazines, videos, cross-dressing, prostitution, affairs, or other actions that seduce him into believing they can fulfill the deep cry within him that is seeking satisfaction through sexual

intensity and release. He may find that even though it is lonely to masturbate to videos, he can be truly himself with the inanimate resource. There
is no risk of intimacy and losing himself. Yet if you struggle with an addiction, you will find that the very avenue to filling the hunger inside you, to
be completely and freely loved for who you are, can be met only as you risk
being true to yourself within the sexual intimacy of your relationship with
your wife.

DISCOVERING INTIMACY IN SEX

To experience the wonderful feeling of truly being yourself during sex
with your wife will bring healing and peace to the loneliness and anxiousness you may carry. You must first be able to relinquish equating her
femaleness with your maleness and heal the destructive relationship patterns that include your personal issues. You will then learn to enjoy sex for
sex and not need sex to be something more than it was intended to be. As
you are able to abandon yourself with your wife and just delight in the
enjoyment of being close, true freedom will flow.

The quality of your sexual intimacy will improve for both you and your
wife as you learn to

- share how you perceive sex and your sexual relationship.
- share how you think and feel about important issues in your relationship in general and in sex specifically.
- listen to and connect with what your wife thinks, feels, and needs.
- actively take responsibility to make your sexual relationship the best
it can be by
  — communicating your sexual desires without either subtle or overt
demand.
  — relinquishing your sexual rights.
  — remembering and responding to your wife's needs, desires, and
pace.
  — interacting verbally and nonverbally during sex as that has been
agreed upon and works best for both of you.
  — soaking in the pleasure of touching and being touched rather than
going for intercourse and release.
  — affirming, validating, and delighting in your wife both personally
and sexually.

Asking this much of you may seem unfair and unattainable. We hope
not. Take one step at a time. When that becomes natural, try the next step.

Before long, sex with your wife will be more than you ever imagined it could be. Long term, you will not suffer. The result of your efforts will be deep sexual fulfillment for both of you.

> *Therefore a man shall leave his father*
> *and mother and be joined to his wife,*
> *and they shall become one flesh*
> (Gen. 2:24).

Chapter 7

When Sex Isn't Working

Men are troubled when sex does not work the way they envision that it should. Yet men are hesitant or even resistant to learn about sex because they believe sex is just supposed to work—without having to learn about it or work to make it work. Harold B. Smith, the executive editor of *Marriage Partnership*, interviewed four men about the sexual side of marriage. Kent responded that his biggest surprise sexually was "the fact that sex didn't just happen. It's complicated" (*Marriage Partnership*, Winter 1993, p. 48).

Attending a seminar on sex, reading a book on sex, or your wife's telling you how she would like sex all imply to you that there must be something wrong that needs to be fixed. You don't take your car to the mechanic if there is not something wrong with it and you don't go to a seminar on sex unless there is something wrong with you. To need advice or help suggests inadequacy. John Gray comments on this point:

> The most frequently expressed complaint men have about women is that women are always trying to change them. . . . Their sense of self is defined through their ability to achieve results. . . . To offer a man unsolicited advice is to presume that he doesn't know what to do or that he can't do it on his own. Asking for help . . . is perceived as a sign of weakness (*Men Are from Mars, Women Are from Venus*, pp. 15, 16, 17).

However, women are often eager to read a book on sex or go to a seminar on sexual relationships. Even though women are supposedly less interested in sex than men are, they are very interested, maybe even more interested than men, in improving the relationship quality of sex and moving toward greater intimacy with their spouses.

Just as a man's sense of self is evaluated through achievement of results, a woman gets her sense of self by being affirmed in her relationships. So when your wife wants you to read this book or this chapter, she is searching to improve her sexual relationship with you in order to feel better about herself. Yet her interest in making sex better can feel as if she is trying to improve you, which means there is something wrong with you that needs improvement. Your sense of self may be challenged by her need to build her sense of self.

WHAT CAN YOU DO?

You can know that God ordained this wonderful gift of sex and set both of your bodies in motion to work, but for some reason sex isn't quite happening the way God meant or the way you or she expected. What has interrupted that natural design?

Know Why It Isn't Working

What is going on when sex isn't working? Simply put, the natural interest and the natural experience of pleasure somehow are outweighed by the concern, conflict, or anxiety that blocks the natural flow of the feelings or responses. Neither of you will want to do something on a regular basis that is aversive, negative, or doesn't work. So unless sex stays on the pleasurable side of the dial, one of you will avoid it or be frustrated by it.

――――― ◆ ◆ ◆ ―――――

When sex is not working,
the natural flow of feelings and responses
is blocked by concern, conflict, or anxiety.

――――― ◆ ◆ ◆ ―――――

Anxiety

When anxiety interrupts sexual pleasure, performance demands are the basis for the sexual dilemma. Fear may be the source of your anxiety. You may feel anxious during sex or in anticipation of sex because of your fear of failure or fear of not measuring up to some standard. Anxiety tends to perpetuate itself. The more you fear, the more anxious you are in sex, and the less you are able to perform during sex. You become a slave to anxiety.

Bob Buford wrote about "Success Panic" in *Halftime*: "It snuck in like a thief in the night—a quiet, insidious intruder disturbing the dark peace and slinking about to pick at the trappings of a life overflowing with contentment, money, achievement, and energy" (p. 45). Sexual anxiety sneaks into a full sexual relationship in much the same way. Sexual anxiety can become your master; you can become a prisoner in your own body, and sex will not work for you. You can release yourself from your imprisonment by abandoning your sexual performance goals and focusing on pleasure and closeness rather than success and results.

Life Circumstances

Life circumstances can have a major effect on what happens in bed. Other pressures can use up sexual energy. If you are finishing a degree, building a business, or starting a profession, if you are unemployed, distracted by illness, concerned about your parents or your children, or preoccupied with your health, you likely will have less energy for sex. Since energy for sex is the same energy basis needed for life, the best way to handle external distractions is to note them, make a plan for how to stay sexually connected even while the life circumstances continue to drain you, and save some time and energy for the two of you.

Past Experience

Your past exerts the most powerful influence on your sexual life. It can haunt you long after the conscious consequences of the past are obvious. A vivid illustration would be the impact from having been exposed to sexual activity too early. Your sexual intensity may have been stirred up before you were developmentally ready to handle sexual exposure or resist victimization. Such violation of innocence will negatively affect your sexual relationship in marriage until you get appropriate professional help.

Relationship Issues

Destructive relationship patterns infiltrate and wear on the very fabric of a couple's sexual life together. Relational sexual turmoil grows out of the kind of problems each of you brought to your marriage. The dynamics of your relationship developed by how your uniquenesses interacted. Since the focus of this book is on you, the man, consider the dilemmas that are due to you and ways that you can make a difference in your sexual life by examining the personal issues.

Get Help

All couples experience temporary disruption of their sexual lives from time to time. We have struggled with several bouts of difficulty. The first was after our honeymoon. Joyce's enthusiastic pursuit of Cliff probably triggered performance pressure. That was quickly alleviated when Joyce backed off. The next dilemma was pain for Joyce after our first child was born. That pain continued and caused decreased interest until after our second child was born twenty-two months later. Counting ejaculations after a vasectomy revisited the performance pressure of our early marriage for Cliff. And then there have been periods when outside life pressures have caused dry spells. You may have struggled with similar difficulties that the two of you were able to identify and correct without professional help. Such struggles are normal.

─────── ◆ ◆ ◆ ───────

Temporary disruption of sexual functioning is normal.

─────── ◆ ◆ ◆ ───────

When the pattern of disruption persists longer than a month or two, it is probably time to seek outside help. Remember, asking for help is perceived by many men as a sign of weakness. It may be hard for you to stop and ask for directions to a specific address. It will be much more difficult to ask for sexual direction. And yet the amount of pain that you will avoid will be well worth it. As a sexual struggle invades your relationship, it will also affect your and your wife's self-esteem. As you feel worse about yourselves, each will respond with characteristic weaknesses. You may withdraw, become more aggressive, communicate put-downs, show frustration or anger, or in some other way be destructive to your relationship. The cost of asking for help will be greatly repaid by the benefits of getting help.

─────── ◆ ◆ ◆ ───────

Persistent disruption of sexual functioning will require outside intervention. The cost of going for help will be repaid by the benefits of that help.

─────── ◆ ◆ ◆ ───────

Sexual dilemmas have a way of perpetuating themselves. Long after the initial cause of the difficulty has passed, the predicament may persist. Failure elicits more failure. Spouses avoid each other because they don't want to have repeat failure experiences. When they finally do connect, it has been a long time since the last experience, and both are more anxious and feel more pressure to succeed. The likelihood of success lessens, and the problem becomes greater. The self-perpetuating nature of sexual difficulties makes it absolutely essential to get outside assessment and direction.

◆ ◆ ◆

Sexual failure perpetuates
more failure; intervention interrupts failure.

◆ ◆ ◆

TWENTY-ONE WAYS NOT TO LOVE YOUR LOVER

#1: The Naive Lover

If you were one of those kids who was shy, withdrawn, or restricted from the usual bumbling activities of learning how to connect with girls when you were in junior high, you may fit the description of the naive lover. Those earlier years of learning how to be you with those giggly, developing junior high girls were essential to growing up. Even though those years from age eleven to fifteen were awkward, they were basic to learning to be a sexual man.

High school and college dating either helped you overcome any awkwardness you did not master in junior high or left you confirmed with your discomfort relating to women. If in high school you had a date only for the high school prom and were focused on sports, cars, computers, or electronics, your naivete continued. Then in college if you focused on your engineering or accounting interests rather than dating, you did not come to your marriageable years with much confidence or security.

When you finally did snag and marry your wife, you may have felt awkward in your physical interaction with her. Being sexual did not flow easily for you. You hadn't spent a lot of time kissing, so passionate kissing left you uncomfortable and her wanting. There may have been a kind of modesty that you felt or still feel. Your wife may sometimes give you the message, even though she is kind about it, that you don't quite know what you're doing. You don't know how to be with a woman in a way that satisfies her sexually.

If this describes you, take heart. The fastest learners that we work with in sexual therapy are the naive men. You come like an empty sponge ready to soak up anything that you can learn. Many self-help resources are available. You and your wife can work through a book such as our *Restoring the Pleasure*. But for you, the sexual retraining section will be a sexual training. A video series such as *The Magic and Mystery of Sex* will give you four hours of education and modeling and help you develop ways to talk. (See the order form in the back of the book.) Attend a seminar on sexuality to saturate yourself with input, and speed up your learning curve. Both you and your wife will be delighted with the rewards of learning fast and retaining what you have learned.

#2: The Goal-Oriented Lover

The first type of goal-oriented lover is the man who leads a goal-oriented life. His daily calendar is his god. He is likely an entrepreneur. By that, we mean that he sets his goals, works toward them, accomplishes them, and then moves on to new goals. Marriage may have been one of those goals. That is, he set out to find a wonderful wife, court her in style, get his family and home established, and now he has moved on to the next project.

Entrepreneurialism may work well when you're starting a company or building a church, but your wife will likely be unhappy to be the project left behind. She will feel left out.

If you are going to have a marriage and a sexually fulfilling relationship as part of that marriage, you need to modify your goal orientedness. Make your entrepreneurial style work for you rather than against you. You have to make your relationship with your wife a priority. Make the decision that you are going to be a lover to your wife. Design into your life the amount of connecting time and sharing time that will serve her and maintain a joyful sexual life. Plan these times for you and your wife in your schedule. (Do the same for your family.) Follow our recommendation of fifteen minutes per day, one evening per week, one day per month, and one weekend per season.

The second type of goal-oriented lover is the watchful lover. He watches to see if she is getting aroused, if she is lubricating, if her nipples are erect, if he has an erection, if sex is taking too long, if she is reaching the same level of ecstasy that she has in the past, if she is getting him excited in the way that he wants her to get him excited, if she has had an orgasm or four orgasms. All of these goals get in the way of the natural loving, connecting process of two people becoming one.

To change your habits if you are a watchful, goal-oriented lover will require an entire shift in approach and mentality. It is a shift from watching whether you are achieving the goals to getting lost in the pleasure. When you can indeed enjoy sex for mutual pleasure, then the importance of the goals drops off because the goal is pleasure.

Dan, another man Harold Smith interviewed on sex in marriage, said he was improving his sex life by "learning that Jeannie's not as hung up on performance as I am. I'm more analytical, wondering, 'Was it good for both of us? Why was it good?' She, on the other hand, seems to be more satisfied sexually because it's sex with me. . . . Maybe it means whatever happens physically between us is good sex" (*Marriage Partnership*, Winter 1993, p. 52).

#3: The Bored Lover

Sex may have become routine, and you are bored with the repetitiveness of your sex life. The way you made love five years ago or fifteen years ago is no different from the way you do it today. You see yourself as a singularly uncreative person. You want to change, but you're unduly modest and have no ideas on how you would experiment even if you felt the freedom to do so. You have repeated the same steps of lovemaking time after time because doing anything different would make you feel vulnerable and anxious.

For you, change will have to be deliberate. Start by talking about your concern with your wife, and then come up with a plan, however simple it may be. Sometimes even shifting which way you lie in bed so that your head is at the foot of the bed can bring a whole new perspective. A change in location can provide new spark. You might make love on the floor or in the guest bedroom or on the patio. Changing which one of you is the active one will make a major difference. If you need suggestions, our book *52 Ways to Have Fun, Fantastic Sex* will provide one new sexual adventure per week.

If you find you cannot take any steps to add new spark to your sex life because the efforts require too much vulnerability, you may need to do some self-exploration. You may pursue writing or journaling or individual psychotherapy to help you open yourself up to the one person in the world that you've committed to share yourself with at this deep level.

#4: The Insecure Lover

Insecure lovers struggle with low self-esteem, which grows out of the emotional needs they brought from their family of origin, a physical or appearance disability, a lack of educational or vocational success, or hurts from past relationships. Men who do not feel good about themselves respond in one direction or the other. Either they are passive and compliant, never expressing their needs or expectations, or they are directly or indirectly demanding and insistent, as we discussed in the previous chapter. Neither leaves the woman feeling the quiet confidence that she is looking for in the man she loves.

Changing how you feel about yourself can be a lifelong project. Nevertheless, both you and your wife will find immediate relief when you are able to identify that your sexual stresses are due to your insecurity. Once you identify the source of the difficulty, you can consciously work on the aspects of yourself that you can control. You can improve your appearance, vocabulary, habits, or other idiosyncracies, or you can find ways other than sex to get validation. Allowing yourself to be vulnerable enough to share and work with your wife will draw the two of you together and can be the most important step toward becoming a more secure lover.

#5: The Sloppy Lover

The sloppy lover has not learned to care. He may have grown up in a home that did not attend to the refined habits of cultivated living, or he may have rejected his mother's nagging of him to practice sophistication. If you're a sloppy lover, you may be inattentive to your general hygiene and bodily preparation for the sexual experience. The unshowered, unshaven man with poor oral hygiene is rarely appealing to a woman. If you have rationalized that her complaints about you are her problem, you need to understand that *every woman needs a clean man!* Perhaps your sloppiness has to do with your lack of attention to detail in the lovemaking experience. You do not pay attention to where your elbow is landing or what you say or how you move your or her body. You will probably know if you are a sloppy lover by listening to the gentle, or not so gentle, comments that your wife has made.

Our advice would be to do something about your sloppiness, and do it now! You will not talk your wife into accepting your sloppiness as just a part of your wonderful quirky personality. Whether you lack good hygiene and preparation or you make insensitive comments or actions, you need to recognize the sloppiness that bothers your wife and make the changes that are necessary for her. She needs to be able to talk to you about your bothersome habits, no matter how embarrassing that might be. And you need to start being more careful, by decision, not because you feel like practicing these important routines. Your taking actions of care will help your wife feel that you value her. The wife of the sloppy lover feels uncared for, disregarded, and devalued.

#6: The Codependent Lover

The codependent label became popular and overused about ten years ago, but it is helpful here. The codependent person feeds off another person's pathology. The codependent husband keeps his wife's resistance to sex going by his grumbling and complaining about her lack of desire. She "needs" him to be grumbling or negative toward her so that she doesn't want to have sex with him, and he "needs" her to be sexually resistant so he can grumble and complain. It is almost a dance.

You may recognize the pattern that has been established between the two of you. Each of you plays your part and knows it well. You almost wouldn't know how to function without the ongoing provocation or complaint or sadness that seems to be there between you. If you are unhappy with your sexual relationship and you blame each other, you probably are perpetuating your sexual pattern with your codependent needs to keep it going. The sexual difficulty serves some purpose for you, even though you are adamant that you do not like things the way they are.

Since the pattern feeds itself, it is difficult to break. For us as sexual therapists, the challenge is to get both spouses' sides of the pattern under control at the same time and long enough for each to see hope for change. As a husband, you could bring change by stopping your negativity and starting to affirm your wife. Focus on any positive, no matter how small or insignificant her efforts may seem to you. Almost inevitably, her sexual resistance will decrease. A negative, complaining, and derogatory husband will produce a resistant wife. By stopping your complaints, you give her no excuse to resist. You may need the help of a quick, sharp, strong therapist.

#7: The Avoidant Lover

The avoidant lover is sometimes quite unsure of himself. He may be naive as we talked about in #1. He may have been hurt in a past situation.

He may be self-conscious about his body or his penis size. Concern about penis size begins in preadolescence and can continue into adulthood. Penis size has little or nothing to do with a man's ability to satisfy a woman since a woman's vagina is a muscle that can accommodate any size penis and the pleasurable sensations are only in the lower one and one-half to two inches of the vagina. Besides, erect penises are all close to equal. Nevertheless, apprehension about penis size is one reason a man avoids his wife. Still another reason is fear of being vulnerable with a woman. It may seem too much of an emotional risk to reach out and engage in a sexual experience. He may rather reach for the remote!

So where's the remote?

If initiation—that is, who gets the sexual experience started—is an issue for the two of you and your wife is angry with you for not meeting her sexual needs, you may be an avoidant lover. If you have difficulty initiating any kind of interpersonal contact, initiating sex will be particularly difficult. Your avoidance is likely to affect your wife by triggering anxiety and anger in her about not getting her sexual needs met. She will probably become pursuant and demanding of sex, which will only exaggerate your need to pull away. The pattern is another circular, self-perpetuating system that creates distance. But in some ways, that is what you want because closeness is uncomfortable.

A man who avoids the interpersonal stress of approaching his wife for sex may use masturbation as the sexual outlet. Masturbation is much less hassle, you don't fear rejection, you're less likely to fail, and you don't have to risk intimacy. You may have lived alone for years and found your sexual fulfillment through masturbation. You long for at the same time that you fear sexual intimacy.

Your avoidance will not change without conscious and deliberate effort. Your wife needs to stop pursuing; you need to initiate sexual contact, by decision, on a designated, regular basis. You cannot wait until you feel like initiating sex with your wife.

All masturbation must stop. You cannot masturbate under any circumstances. You must force yourself to relinquish that form of self-satisfaction so that your bodily urges will nudge you to take action with your wife.

If sex with your wife has seemed like too much work, talk with her about your conditions for pleasure. Build self-assurance and comfort with intimacy and initiation through a planned system of sexual contact. You can change from being an avoidant lover.

#8: The Lazy Lover

Maturity brings the realization that effort and delay of immediate gratification for the long-term benefit work best in life. A man may not have learned this in general or may not have developed this pattern in his sexual life.

If the effort of connecting with your wife and the delay of your ejaculation are not worth the long-term benefits of a mutually satisfying sexual relationship, you are probably a lazy lover. Is it just too much of a hassle to talk with her, touch her and get her feeling good about you, stroke her body in general, and then stimulate her clitoris for twenty minutes? You are not willing to go through what it takes. You would like it best if you could give her a cursory rub and then the proverbial "wham, bam, thank you, ma'am." You are even happier if you get an ejaculation, and you don't even have to worry about sexual satisfaction for her. There is no mutual pleasure, and your laziness absolutely precludes any possibility of bonding or deep connection. You will not have a deeply satisfying sexual life because you have not been willing to exert the effort or take the time to see to it that her physical and deeper emotional needs are met.

Your lack of motivation will be the biggest barrier to changing your lazy lover pattern. You have to decide to go against what is natural for you. You have to pick yourself up by your own bootstraps and decide to take a few small steps toward the goal of changing your patterns. To find true ongoing fulfillment, you have to decide to delay immediate gratification for the deeper satisfaction.

He went that-a-way!

You and your wife would do best to write out a step-by-step plan listing the requirements for all sexual encounters. For example, you might specify that you spend twenty minutes in talking before you do any touching and then you spend ten minutes of general kissing and caressing before you take off any clothes. Define very specific behavioral expectations that are timed by an electronic timer. Normally, we are against a step one, two, three approach to sex, but for the lazy lover, a specific design planned with your wife will bring amazing benefits.

#9: The Angry Lover

Anger could be coming from two totally different parts of your being. You may have brought old anger from your past into your marriage. Anger—toward your parents, siblings, schoolmates, the army, a boss, God, or whoever—may have been eating at you for years. Or the anger may stem from your relationship. The hurts, the frustrations, or the fears that have plagued your marriage may never have been dealt with in such a way that you can move away from them and feel free of their impact. The residual of that relationship anger finds its way into your marriage bed. You may express that anger directly with hurtful or critical comments or actions, or you may express it more passively by creating sexual distance.

A flare of intense emotion—momentary anger or irritation—can keep aliveness and intensity in the relationship. Anger and sexual passion reside next to each other; one can trigger the other. Anger may be thought of as the dark side of passion. Intensity and expression of the hurt, frustration, or fear behind the anger can actually lead to greater passion and intimacy. But using anger to get passion can be destructive.

An anger problem is best worked out with a therapist and not taken to bed. We highly recommend Dr. Neil Clark Warren's book *Make Anger Your Ally*. You can work through the process of identifying the type and source of your anger and learn how to use that energy for your benefit rather than express it in ways that are destructive both to you and to your relationship.

If your anger leads to either verbal or physical abuse or causes you to be hurtful in the sexual experience, you must get help immediately. Anger that is out of control and being used to hurt is a serious crisis. Intervention is necessary to change the destructive pattern forever. It is never right, helpful, justified, or permissible for anger to come out in ways that demean or harm.

#10: The Possessive Lover

The possessive lover is the jealous lover. Unchecked jealousy creeps into the inner being and eats away at it like fresh wood termites on a sycamore tree. It eats at your core. Jealousy stifles love and interrupts the natural flow of sexual abandonment. Your wife is not yours to possess; she is a gift of God to freely enjoy, delight in, and give yourself to. She chose you, and she is committed to you. But sexually, she needs to be free to give herself to you—to carry out the instruction that each spouse's body is the other's. She cannot freely say, "Yes," without being totally free to say, "No."

◆ ◆ ◆

She cannot freely say, "Yes," to sex
until she can freely say, "No."

◆ ◆ ◆

What is your jealousy or possessiveness about? Husbands let jealousy interfere with their sex lives for a number of reasons.

A husband's most common preoccupation is with a prior lover that his wife had before they were married or even before they knew each other. We hear this every day in our offices, and it validates to us God's standard of saving sex for marriage. The couple may have been married for ten years, but the husband is still haunted by the thought of his wife's having been with someone else. During sex, any pause in her action, any apparent lack of enthusiasm, any shift from how she usually is, can trigger his jealous concern. He may be preoccupied with and obsessed with getting the details of her history. It may seem impossible for him to leave her past buried where it needs to be.

The husband's jealousies may be more current. Perhaps he is preoccupied with his wife's boss, her choir director, her teacher, or her tennis instructor. The preoccupation is not based on any inappropriateness between these men and his wife; it stems only from his own anxiety. He may even be jealous of the children, her mother, or her best friend. He focuses on how much of her time they take or how much of her attention they get. He can't seem to help thinking about and commenting on how these people are part of her inner world and in some form replacing him. Unless he feels he is the center of her life, as a child should be to his mother, he becomes anxious.

A couple contacted us to talk about the husband's struggle with possessive jealousy since the inception of their marriage fourteen years ago. Tom was still preoccupied with her sexual activity with a man before she had made a commitment to Christ and prior to meeting and dating Tom. Regularly, Tom reviewed with Brenda the activities of that past involvement. He asked for details, and he was concerned that he not have any future surprises. She anxiously tried to appease him and hoped she had not missed giving him any information that she might remember in the future. After every sexual experience, Tom doubted that their time had been as good as hers with the previous man. Tom's inappropriate obsession was destroying the joy he could have been experiencing with his wife because he feared he could not measure up to her previous sexual partner and could not trust Brenda to be faithful. We had to help Tom accept that Brenda had been cleansed spiritually and mentally from her past. His jealousy about her past was the only current difficulty with that past.

When a husband's possessiveness is not about what the woman is actually doing, it is about the lack of trust and the insecurity he brought into the relationship. If you are such a husband, you must, for the sake of your marriage, get control of that jealousy. If you do not, you will reap the exact opposite of what you desperately desire. You will drive your wife away rather than draw her to you, and the cancer of your jealousy will eat at your soul and destroy you. Seek help to get an understanding of the background source of your possessiveness than rather than focusing on your wife. The security of commitment brings sexual freedom in marriage; possessiveness stifles sexual expressiveness in marriage.

◆ ◆ ◆

The security of commitment
brings sexual freedom;
possessiveness stifles sexual expressiveness.

◆ ◆ ◆

#11: The Selfish Lover

The selfish lover is the actively self-centered lover. He is usually not only selfish in bed but also selfish in life. If you focus on your needs and have difficulty getting with your wife's needs, you are probably a selfish lover. Listen to your words. Do you express "I need," "I want," "you should," "if only you would"? Maybe you just think of yourself as knowing what you want and having refined taste. You believe that if you can get her to meet your needs, you can be free to meet hers. The selfish lover has a "me first" attitude. You may be convinced that you can give to her only when you have first been given to. The "me first" approach to sex with your wife is a direct contradiction to what we believe works best in the sexual relationship in marriage; sex will be the best for both of you when you are the servant leader, the servant lover, and the servant husband.

Repentance and a change of attitude are necessary for reversing this pattern. Selfish habits die slowly unless the habits are submitted to the Christ on the throne of your life. Your wife can also be a big help. Set aside a time to hear in a nondefensive hearing what it is like to be connected with you as a selfish lover. If you can face yourself, you may then have the knowledge, the courage, and the strength, with God's help, to change this selfish nature.

◆ ◆ ◆

With determination, God's help, and your
wife's help, you can relinquish selfish habits.

◆ ◆ ◆

#12: The Passive Lover

The passive lover is the inactive self-centered lover. He says, "Let her do it." This husband has very little capacity to give; he wants to be pleased. He is a one-way sponge; he can only take in. The picture of the passive lover is the description one woman gave of her husband who would prepare for lovemaking by lying down on the bed, putting his hands behind his head, and signaling her that he was ready for her to begin.

The passive lover believes he is special, so he needs to be ministered to or attended to in a unique and special way. There is a touch of royalty in this kind of passive self-centeredness. He may feel that his wife is lucky to have him—someone so charming, so bright, so attractive, so intelligent, so rich, so musical, or whatever special quality he brings. She should be grateful, and if she isn't, lots of other women would be. He may have learned that his specialness was above others and that he had no obligation to give to others or care about their needs and feelings.

This inactive self-centeredness has a way of making others, especially the wife, feel quite inadequate and eventually very angry. Initially, the wife of the passive lover tries to please, but she reaches the point of utter despair or incredibly volatile anger. She feels violated.

Just as the selfish lover requires a change of heart, so does the passive lover. If you are a passive lover, your beliefs about yourself need to change. You cannot continue to assume that you are special and exempt from the normal expectations of the husband-wife relationship. Your false suppositions have been the very antithesis of the servant leader. It is not an easy system to break, but it is absolutely essential if you are going to have a fulfilling sexual life.

◆ ◆ ◆

You are special, but so is your wife; relinquish your rights to be served and serve her.

◆ ◆ ◆

#13: The Critical Lover

The critical lover is evaluative, with a hostile edge. The critical lover's evaluation has a bite to it. His criticalness may not be limited to sex. He may be critical of her housekeeping, her appearance, her weight, her clothes, her decorating, her child rearing, or the way she irons trousers. During sex, he is critical of how she moves or doesn't move in bed, whether or not she shows the right degree of enthusiasm, or whether she responds at the right speed. The critical lover evaluates in all these ways. This negative, evaluative process stifles spontaneity and joy.

If you are a critical lover, evaluating with a bite is automatic. Perhaps one of your parents was that way with you.

Correcting your critical nature may start by controlling your tongue before you get control of your mind. You need to make a conscious and deliberate decision not to say what you think. It would be better not to say anything than to say something critical. Practice replacing the critical thought with a positive message. You may argue that you would be deceptive. However, critical thoughts expressed multiply the severity of their impact and perpetuate the habit of negative thinking. The promise of honesty with each other doesn't include that you share every negative thought or feeling. The promise of honesty only guarantees that what you say is true. As your wife hears positives from you, you will be rewarded by her enjoyment, which will elicit more positives from you. Eventually, even your thinking will be less critical.

Your tongue is the solution to your critical nature; you can control it!

#14: The Controlling Lover

The controlling lover obviously needs to be in control. He needs to control his wife; he needs to control the sequence; he needs to control the activities; he often even needs to control the response. Sex has to be on his terms. If not, he gets anxious and sabotages the experience.

Your need for control may be specific to certain aspects of the sexual experience or only become an issue when you feel that your wife or the event is not in control. Maybe the only time you need control is when you're anxious or insecure about your response or about your performance. As you feel more shaky, you manage the shakiness by getting a firmer grip on the sexual experience—you take charge.

Whatever your need for control, if you happen to be a controlling lover, the likelihood is that you are getting one of two responses. Either your wife is passively going along with your control and losing interest, or she is fighting you for control every step of the way.

Letting go of control may be tough for you to do. Start by identifying what triggers your need for control. Talk about your awareness with your wife. Have fun experimenting with her taking charge of an entire sexual experience. Tell her your thoughts as you are in the passive role. Make an agreement that each of you will let the other know when you sense that your control is taking charge of your sex life. As you learn to focus on mutual pleasure and release your firm grip, you will discover the release that comes with being able to let go of the control.

———— ◆ ◆ ◆ ————

You can use your need for control;
take charge and provide structure
to let go of control.

◆ ◆ ◆

#15: The Distant Lover

The distant lover avoids intimacy; he remains aloof. The distant lover has to keep his distance not only from his wife but also from himself. The Scriptures speak a very real truth when they say that you are to love others as you love yourself. You could even reverse that and say you are able to love others only as you are able to love or accept yourself.

The distant lover struggles with a lack of self-acceptance, which he has learned to manage by a projection of aloofness. He may falsely be seen as self-confident or even stuck up, but his standoffishness is about his discomfort with intimacy. Intimacy is the deep knowing of each other because spouses can be their true selves together. A distant lover does not have that capacity.

There is usually a good reason why a lover is distant. You may have experienced either pain or coldness from your parents while you were growing up. You may have been hurt when you allowed yourself to be open in a previous relationship. You may have encountered negative, hurtful peers during your childhood years. Whatever the reason, your distance interferes. You may show your discomfort with intimacy by regularly asking questions of your wife during lovemaking. With you in the inquiring role and her in the respondent role, you keep a safe distance. Your relationship cannot survive your distance!

Your spouse will be reluctant to talk to you about her longing for closeness with you because she fears more distance. She may fear that her confrontation of you will change your cordial distance to a colder distance. So, be aware of how the very nature of your distancing makes attempts at getting close to you perplexing for her.

First of all, you need to be able to get in touch with yourself and know who you are and accept yourself so that you can share yourself freely with your wife. You must learn to break down the barriers surrounding your heart to keep you safe. Then you will be able to let her get close to you and allow yourself to get close to her.

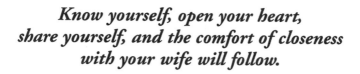

Know yourself, open your heart,
share yourself, and the comfort of closeness
with your wife will follow.

#16: The Inhibited Lover

Inhibition takes on many forms. The inhibition could involve talking about sex, sharing his body, responding sexually, communicating his feelings, being touched, or having his sexual parts fondled, or letting himself experience these dimensions of his wife. He may be hesitant to make noise, touch his wife's genitals, enjoy her lubrication, or express his needs and desires.

You can move from your inhibitions
to freedom; take one
step at a time.

If you are an inhibited lover, your wife will know it. She won't know how to talk to you about your inhibitions and help you past them. You can overcome the restrictions your inhibitions place on both you and your wife. With your wife, define your inhibitions very specifically. Write them on one side of a blank piece of paper. On the other side, write what total freedom from your inhibitions would be like. Then break down in small steps the actions you would take to get from where you are to total freedom with your wife. Below is a diagram of what we are suggesting here.

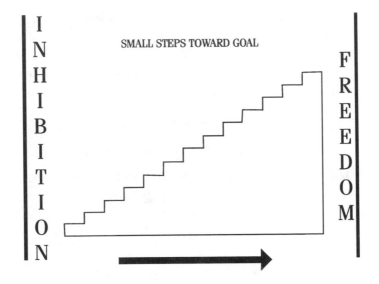

#17: The Power-Needy Lover

The power-needy lover is similar to the controlling lover except that the primary emphasis is on exerting power rather than control. He has a need for domination. He cannot respond when he is not feeling more powerful than his wife. When she pursues, he rejects. He needs her to give in to his asking for experiences or events that he knows are difficult for her or at a time that is difficult for her. He sets up a power struggle that he must win.

A man with this need for power usually had a mix of power struggles with both parents. Mother may have dominated and controlled or not been there for you. Father probably controlled with his greater physical prowess. He may have beat you and shamed you. If you become anxious or upset when you don't have the power, try to talk to the little boy in you. Let the little boy know he no longer needs to protect himself against Mom's or Dad's control. You have a wife who can be your companion if you will allow her equality with you.

To break your need for power, you need to understand your issues as they relate to women, identify your specific patterns with your wife, and then counteract both with your actions. Your behaviors will precede your feelings. Change will happen as a result of your choice to change. As you relinquish power with your actions, your need for power will diminish, and your feelings of comfort even when you are not the power person will grow.

———— ◆ ◆ ◆ ————

As you choose to relinquish power,
your need for power will diminish, and
your comfort with not being in power
will grow.

———— ◆ ◆ ◆ ————

#18: The Disinterested Lover

Men are touted as always interested and always eager for sex; a man's lack of interest may make him feel unmanly. Men's struggle with low sexual desire is more common than most people believe, and much has been written about it. Inevitably, the lack of frequency is troubling to the wife who is eager to be desired and fulfilled sexually.

Since there may be many causes for low sexual desire, your primary focus has to be on understanding what your disinterest is about. We've already talked about the lack of sexual interest or pursuit of the naive lover, the bored lover, the insecure lover, and the avoidant lover. You may have identified with one of these ways not to love your lover. You may have come from a home lacking in intimacy. You did not learn to be close or to share yourself, so sexual connection is an unnatural process for you. You may have been a victim of sexual abuse or trauma. You may have been raised in a rigid antisexual environment or by a controlling and dominant mother who demeaned men, especially your father. You may struggle with an addiction or homosexual fantasies or desires that interfere with your desire for your wife. Any of these conditions could be reasons for you to struggle with lack of sexual desire.

Situational circumstances could temporarily interfere with your desire for sex. Preoccupation with stress on the job, with children, or with finances could get in the way. Depression, anxiety, or phobias may hinder, especially if they are sexual phobias. Illness, alcohol, prescription drugs, or hormonal disruptions may be physical bases for your lack of sexual interest. Relationship conflicts in your marriage can temporarily halt your sexual desire for your wife. When situational events are relieved, sexual desire usually returns.

If your lack of desire is due to feelings of sexual inadequacy or deeper emotional issues or trauma, we suggest sexual therapy and psychotherapy. If yours is a relationship issue, marital therapy is needed. Help is available. You can do something about your sexual disinterest; take it on and be deliberate, conscious, and intentional about changing it. Your biggest hurdle to overcome will be your disinterest in doing something about your sexual disinterest.

———— ◆ ◆ ◆ ————

You can determine to counteract
your sexual disinterest
and become sexual
with your wife.

———— ◆ ◆ ◆ ————

#19: The Hasty Lover

The man who rushes sex may be insecure, anxious, goal oriented, or not in control of his ejaculation. He may think of himself as the seven-minute wonder. His wife may think of him as selfish. He can learn to extend sexual pleasure for both him and his wife and become the marathon wonder!

If ejaculatory control is your struggle, you are not alone. Of the couples who attend our sexual enhancement seminars, one-third to one-half of the men want to learn how to last longer.

The man who does not have control of ejaculation ejaculates during the preliminary play or within seconds or minutes after entry. He cannot allow enough time for his wife to respond. This is a habit you may have learned during your rushed adolescence or young adult masturbation. Or you may never have learned to attend to the level of your arousal so that you can control it before you get to the point of ejaculation.

You can learn to control ejaculation, even as you learned bladder control as a child. Give yourself a couple of months and the determination to follow the steps outlined in one of two methods. In her book *PE: How to Overcome Premature Ejaculation*, Helen Singer Kaplan teaches you how to attend to and manage your levels of arousal by stopping and starting genital stimulation. You can do this by yourself or with your wife. In *Restoring the Pleasure*, we have step-by-step instructions for learning ejaculatory control using the squeeze technique. Both methods teach you to condition your body to extend the length of your preorgasmic arousal for longer and longer periods of time. We encourage you to attend to this with real vigor, devoting yourself diligently to the process of learning, which we believe every man can do. You will discover greater passion, intensity, and sexual fulfillment as you last longer.

◆ ◆ ◆

You can learn to extend preorgasmic arousal and heighten your passion, intensity, and sexual fulfillment.

◆ ◆ ◆

#20: The Anxious Lover

Anxiety in lovemaking interferes with pleasure and functioning. A man's self-consciousness, watchfulness, monitoring, or spectatoring gets him focused on the event, on his actions, and on his wife's actions rather than on the enjoyment of the pleasure. If the anxiety continues, it will interfere with his erectile functioning and can hinder him from carrying out the sexual act because of his difficulty getting or keeping an erection.

When anxiety is the source of erectile dysfunction, anxiety interferes with the natural bodily response much like anxiety can cause insomnia. You cannot just decide to fall asleep at a given moment as you can decide to move your elbow or shout at someone. Rather, given the right conditions, you will fall asleep when you are tired. Getting and keeping an erection are similar. If you attend to an erection, concentrate on it, or try to get one, your efforts will keep it from happening. But if you provide the right conditions and are aroused, an erection will occur naturally.

So what does the anxious lover need to do? Make sure your anxiety about getting or keeping erections has nothing to do with a physical problem causing your erectile difficulty. You need to have a physical examination that tests penile blood pressure, nighttime erections, hormonal levels, and medication side effects. If you have no physical reason for your problem with erections, you need to learn to distract from focusing on performance and refocus on the delightful, pleasurable, skin-to-skin touch.

To make the switch from anxious loving focused on performance to pleasurable loving focused on sensations, you must rule out intercourse or attempts at intercourse. Your wife must learn to enjoy your body and allow you to enjoy hers without demand for response. You also need to be free to tell your wife when you are anxious about your response. If a self-help approach is not enough, you may need the help of a sexual therapist. You can learn to enjoy sex without anxiety and without demanding an erection.

———— ◆ ◆ ◆ ————

You can learn to enjoy sex
without anxiety or demand
for an erection.

———— ◆ ◆ ◆ ————

#21: The Addicted Lover

If sex controls a man rather than his having control of sex, he is sexually addicted. He depends on sexual gratification to feel good and survive. His addicted sexual behavior, which is connected with anxiety and guilt, is a compulsion.

Your addictive sexual behavior pattern likely has a cycle that begins with preoccupation. Your preoccupation with thoughts and a desire to act builds until you begin your addictive rituals. Your ritual may include rationalizations. You convince yourself that your actions will not hurt anyone, no one will know, you deserve it, your wife is not meeting your needs, or you justify "good" coming from what you intend to do. You disconnect from your typical way of thinking; you zone out. Preparatory activities may be part of your ritual that leads to acting out. Then you act. The actual behavior may include watching pornography on videos or cable TV, visiting a massage parlor, propositioning a prostitute, having an affair, peeping, cross-dressing, molesting, masturbating, or demanding certain types of sexual activities with your wife. It can happen in your home or in public. Whatever the behavior, it virtually always includes sexual release. With the release come relief and then despair and remorse, followed by the resolve never to act again. The resolve lasts only so long before the cycle starts over again. It may be a cycle that you repeat several times a day or only several times a year.

You know whether you are addicted. Your wife probably knows, too, even if she has not been fully able to admit it to herself. If you engage in troublesome sexual practices that are wrong, but you can stop them if you choose to, you are violating your relationship with God and your wife; however, you are not addicted. If you are an addicted lover, you are hooked and cannot stop yourself. Your behavior is destructive to yourself and destructive to your relationship because you are choosing sex in some other form over your wife. You are violating 1 Corinthians 7:3–5. You are not fulfilling your sexual duty to your wife and giving her authority over your body. Your addiction is sin. You will struggle with it for the rest of your life.

Help is available, and help you will need. You can start with our chapter on sexual addictions in *Restoring the Pleasure*, but if you want a full treatment, you might read Dr. Patrick Carnes's book *Out of the Shadows*, or Mark Laaser's book, *The Secret Sin*. Commitment to a twelve-step program will be a necessity.

◆ ◆ ◆

*As a sexual addict, you will always
be an addict, but with the help of God and others,
you can be in control of your addiction
for the rest of your life.*

◆ ◆ ◆

To get and keep control of your addictive behavior, you must face that you are addicted to acting out sexually, know that you will always be an addict who needs help to stay in control, and accept that you need God's forgiveness and His power and accountability to others to conquer your obsession.

WHEN HERS DOESN'T WORK

What are you to do when your wife is struggling in some area of sexual adjustment or fulfillment? You have yourself straightened out, but she is in trouble. What if she just plain isn't interested, or when she is, nothing happens? She doesn't respond. Or maybe having sex always hurts her.

Recognize that if you have taken care of your sexual issues, you are not responsible for the fact that her body is not working. You may be a part of the solution, but you are not the cause. You can help.

◆ ◆ ◆

You are not responsible for
sex not working for your wife,
but you may be vital to the solution.

◆ ◆ ◆

Her Lack of Interest

Women, just like men, lack sexual interest for a variety of reasons. The primary reason a woman is not interested is that sex has been connected with emotional pain, trauma, disappointment, or violation. The event may have been exposure to pornography, explicit sexual touching or other childhood sexual abuse, a traumatic medical genital procedure as a child or adult, or being sexually forced in adulthood. Probably the second most common reason for a woman's decreased desire is a husband who persistently pursues sex. If that was true for you, it will take some time for her to be aware of her own sexuality now that you have backed off. The third, and most tenacious, reason for disinterest is being the product of an alcoholic home, especially an alcoholic father. The daughter of an alcoholic is most resistant and disinterested until she becomes physically aroused. Then she can be very responsive and have an orgasm, but afterward she will quickly shut off any interest. She knows how to be out of control, but she hates the out-of-control feeling that reminds her of her alcoholic home.

A woman lacks interest in sex for other reasons. If the woman feels uncared for or if sex is a mechanical event to give the man his release, she almost inevitably will be disinterested. If she has grown up to believe that pleasure is sinful, desire will be a struggle for her. If she was taught against masturbation or appropriately instructed regarding the wrongs of sex outside marriage without the positive message of sex within marriage and of God-given sexual drives from adolescence to death, she will have had great passion before marriage and lost all desire shortly after marriage. Life and relationship stresses, physical and emotional issues, and medications can also zap natural sexual urges.

Whatever the cause of your wife's disinterest, you can be a major force in the solution. Your sensitivity to what is going on for her will be a huge start. Your goal of getting with her for her, not to get what you want, will open her up to you. Obviously, any badgering or forcing or cajoling must stop. As she feels your care and your love deep in her soul, over time her negative association with sex can change in the direction of becoming a positive. When her sexual responsiveness becomes associated with feeling heard and understood rather than pain, pursuit, or trauma, she will become the pursuer of that positive connection, and desire will build.

――――――― ◆ ◆ ◆ ―――――――

Your ability to care for your wife
is the start to a positive association
between you and her sexual response;
sexual interest will follow.

――――――― ◆ ◆ ◆ ―――――――

Her Difficulty with Arousal

Apart from the impact of hormonal changes, a woman rarely has difficulty with her physical arousal responses of vaginal lubrication and nipple erection. Often, however, she has no awareness of these bodily responses. Her emotions do not keep up with her body. The woman who doesn't feel sexual arousal is usually preoccupied with keeping her husband happy or trying to respond for him. She has not learned to get in tune with her sexual desires and needs.

The woman who has difficulty with arousal will need permission to develop the skill of going after sex for her. You can free her to do that. Free her to go with her inner urges rather than focus on you. Let her know that as long as she is happy, you are happy. She does not need to respond or perform for you. Give her permission to feel her sexuality on her terms. It's important that she not feel any demands from you or a need to please you but is free to connect with her self and what is going on inside her.

You can participate with her as she learns to go after her sexuality at her own pace. You may need to learn to slow way down and focus on pleasure rather than response or results. As you both get the focus off her performance, the likelihood is that she will be free to discover within herself all of that sexual potential just waiting to be expressed. Her sexual intensity has been inhibited by her own caution and by the dynamic between the two of you that keeps her focused on your and her responses rather than on her own pleasure. Remember, you gain your life when you lose it; you get the response when you stop trying for it. Enjoy the delightful experience of working together.

Her Difficulty with Orgasm

A woman who struggles with or is unable to experience an orgasm will usually finish the sexual experience let down or frustrated and will begin to avoid sex. You know how you would feel if you rarely or never ejaculated. Just as there is a buildup of sperm and seminal fluid for the man, the arousal process causes the woman to become engorged and physically ready for the orgasmic response. When response doesn't occur, over time she slows herself down so that she gets less and less aroused and eventually doesn't want sex.

How can you help? Accept that her orgasm will not make you the lover of all lovers. You are not responsible to give her an orgasm, and she is not responsible to have an orgasm for you. The impetus, the desire, the urge, to be orgasmic can come only from her. You can free her so that she does not need to have an orgasm for you, but she knows that you will participate in whatever way you can to allow her the pleasure she desires.

Since she will never have an orgasm by trying, you can encourage her to stop trying, and you can stop trying to give her one. You can enjoy her body for your pleasure rather than for its response and let her know of your ongoing delight with her very being. Her getting active will distract her from her self-consciousness and jump-start her body's natural, involuntary responses. As she is active in enjoying your body, let her know how much you enjoy her pleasuring of you. As you both refocus on the pleasure of the sensations, her pressure for an orgasm will lessen.

Invite her to be the guide as she instructs you and shares with you what her body hungers for. If she doesn't know, experiment together. Try different types of touch in various areas of her body, and have her talk to you about how each touch feels, not the response it produces.

Accept that she is the authority on her body. A man may attempt to be the authority on what will give a woman an orgasm. The fact is, all women are different. What works for one woman has relatively little to do with what is going to be good for this woman. So, she needs to invite and guide you and you follow her lead. Think of your role as a supporting actor in a movie. She has the lead role; she is the star. Your role is to do all that you can to back her up, to support her, to bring her to the place where all of her sexual potential can be realized.

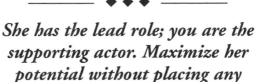

She has the lead role; you are the supporting actor. Maximize her potential without placing any pressure to perform.

Her Pain Interrupts Pleasure

Sex was designed to be a wonderful, enjoyable sensation and experience; it was not meant to hurt. When sex is painful for a woman, a physician may have trouble locating the exact center and source of the pain. Because her genitals look normal upon examination, the woman gets the message, directly or indirectly, that her pain is all in her head. Our response is, "No, it's in her vagina!" After twenty years of treating women who experience painful intercourse, we have never seen a woman who created or imagined her pain. We don't accept the "it's all in the head" approach. Can pain be due to stress? Absolutely. But most often, pain is due to a tight muscle that resulted from past trauma or infection or irritation, it is due to a tear, or there is some other physical basis for the pain. Even if the pain is there due to anxiety and tightness, it still hurts. It still requires physical intervention.

Pain always needs to be taken seriously and at face value.

What can you do? Take her pain seriously. Do not continue the painful experiences. Help her identify and isolate the nature of her pain. Exactly *when* in the experience does the pain occur? Pinpoint *where* the pain occurs. Is it on the outer edge of the vagina, just inside the opening, around the muscle that controls the opening of the vagina, or deep within the vagina? Is it a spot or an area? *What* type of pain is it? Is it a stinging pain or a sharp stabbing pain or a general irritation? Once she is able to answer these questions, she can share the details with her physician who can then be more effective in diagnosing and treating her pain. If she goes to a physician who is unwilling or unable to identify the source of the pain, she should keep looking. She may need to find a vulvar pain specialist. Often this physician has specialized in both gynecology and urology.

Until your wife's pain is relieved, your sexual life together can never be satisfying and fulfilling for both of you. She needs you as her ally in identifying and bringing healing to her pain. There is always an answer, and there is always somebody who can help.

BE THE LOVER OF YOUR WIFE

You can decide what kind of lover you want to be to your wife. Perhaps you saw yourself in bits and pieces in a number of the twenty-one nonlover descriptions. We hope in that process you found ways that you would like to be as a lover and direction and power to take charge of being the lover of all lovers. Your body is not your own; it is hers. As you learn to be a giving and serving lover, you will bring greater love, passion, and intimacy to your marriage and counter the disillusionment that is so often the result of the husband not getting beyond himself and into the wife's world.

To be the lover of lovers to your wife when sex is not working for her does not require you to fix her problem, but you can be a vital part of the solution. Your responsibility is to take her struggle seriously, to back off from your agenda, to get with her, to focus on pleasure, and to get the necessary help to go beyond the specific barrier.

You can make a difference when sex is not working. You can avoid the pitfalls of ineffective lovers, and you can be a part of the solution to her dilemmas. Whether it is some part of you that is not working or some part of her that's not working, defining the issue and applying the recommended solution will always bring the two of you closer together. Your bonus will be a lot more fun in bed with your wife. You will have the delight of a full, unencumbered sexual life together.

It takes wisdom to build a house,
  and understanding to set it on a firm foundation;
It takes knowledge to furnish its rooms
  with fine furniture and beautiful draperies
  (Prov. 24:3, *The Message*).
  Patient persistence pierces through indifference;
    gentle speech breaks down rigid defenses
  (Prov. 25:12, *The Message*).

Chapter 8

Affair Proof Your Marriage

Protecting your marriage and keeping it safe may seem unnecessary to you. You and your wife may be strongly committed to each other and to God. Infidelity isn't an option for either of you. You may be convinced that your love for each other will keep you from being tempted by or attracted to someone of the opposite sex.

> **MYTH:** *If you love your spouse, you will not be tempted by or attracted to someone of the opposite sex.*

Sam and Jenny had been married for twelve years. They viewed their relationship as solid. Their only tension was around sex. Sam had saved himself for marriage, and Jenny's lack of interest really bothered him. Jenny often felt that her only value to Sam was sexual. If she was eager in bed, he was happy. When she was less available and not as involved, he became distant and irritable.

Their children were both in school, so Jenny decided to go back to work part time as an accountant for a large firm. Bill, the accountant who worked next to her, finished divorce proceedings with his wife two months ago. Bill started to ask Jenny questions about how to handle various issues with his children. Jenny found herself sharing more and more with Bill. One day, it hit her: "Bill cares about me as a person. He's not just interested in my body." Probably at that point, the affair started.

UNDERSTAND YOUR VULNERABILITY

INFIDELITY: IT MAY BE IN OUR GENES stood out in bold white-and-gold letters on the black cover of the August 15, 1994, *Time* magazine. The article, written from the perspective of evolutionary psychology, ended with the following sentence: "The first step to being moral is to realize how thoroughly we aren't." Surprise!

Even though you are created in the image of God and are instructed to become one flesh as husband and wife and not to allow the marriage bed to become defiled, you are human. You are a sexual being, and every dimension of your life includes your sexuality.

When the Grass Looks Greener

Once you live with someone day after day, year after year, you tend to see faults. The very characteristics that once intrigued you now irritate. When Jenny seemed hard to get sexually, Sam was challenged to conquer. Initially, when he was so responsive to her body, Jenny responded with excitement. Neither Jenny nor Sam contemplated that newness excites and hides flaws.

─────── ◆ ◆ ◆ ───────

Newness excites and hides flaws.

─────── ◆ ◆ ◆ ───────

The men Harold B. Smith interviewed expressed their struggles that lure them from the reality of sex within marriage:

DAN: The idea of beautiful women who always want you, who are always inviting, who aren't angry with you and whom you won't have to deal with on an emotional level—that's very appealing. And I carried that fantasy into our marriage.

MIKE: I guess my fantasy is to have a woman who wants me so badly she can't keep her hands off me. But that's a fantasy because, one, my wife's not geared that way—although she's geared enough that way that I'm still hoping! And two, I feel that the initiating is my responsibility. I need to court her, to let her know she's desirable to me, to let her know I would love to make love to her. And I think she wants that.

KENT: I was surprised to find out that lust doesn't stop with marriage. If anything, it grows because now you have someone to have sex with and the sensual world around you is saying, "Try this. And now try this!" You somehow think that all of the media images of sexuality should be experienced in your own love life (*Marriage Partnership*, Winter 1993).

Situations Provide Opportunities

Feelings toward a person of the opposite sex may develop when you are in a situation that puts you in frequent or ongoing contact with that person. Attraction and attachment then have the opportunity to grow. It can happen between fellow workers, close friends, neighbors, or boss and employee. It can seem so natural, almost irresistible, and so right!

On the other hand, you can work with some people closely for years, highly respect them, and even really like them but never find yourself attracted in a way that grabs you. That is why it is so important to know yourself and the type of person who triggers your vulnerability.

*Know yourself, and
know your vulnerability.*

Situational attractions happen to some more than to others. Know yourself. If you or your wife tends to be vulnerable to forming attractions or having others become attracted to you, you will need to take more action to safeguard your home fort.

What makes some people more prone to affairs is not totally understood. Some seem to be scanners looking for opportunities. Others seem to give off vibes that attract.

Why feelings happen between two people and not between others is also not clear. Some factors of body chemistry do make a difference.

- Body scent
- Body type
- Emotional type
- Intellectual type

All of these and probably other personal characteristics factor into the complex puzzle of what attracts individuals to each other as friends or lovers. You and your wife should develop an understanding of the types that tend to attract each of you and be particularly alert to being account-able to each other about individuals who are your type.

According to Harville Hendrix in *Getting the Love You Want*, you are more likely to attach to someone you feel has the potential to give you the parental love or affirmation you never received and are now seeking. The person who is attractive to you has to do with finding your parent in that person.

Life Change Increases Vulnerability

As you go through life and its experiences, you develop ways of coping. The older you get, the more set these coping skills become. Any change in life, positive or negative, is a stress in the sense that it jars loose your set toward life. It might be understood as what happens beneath the ground during an earthquake. The magnitude of the earthquake determines the degree of impact. Likewise, the intensity of life change will determine the degree of susceptibility to an outside attachment.

After being a stay-at-home mom and housewife for twelve years, Jenny got a new job. That change increased her openness to Bill's attentiveness. Her eagerness to do well in the workplace, her dressing for work, her new mean-ing in life, and her daily interaction with adults functioning at her level of interest were all conditions of change that increased her vulnerability.

◆ ◆ ◆

Desiring change at home may also increase the likelihood of responding to an attraction.

◆ ◆ ◆

Jenny's response to Bill was heightened by the fact that she wanted Sam to share with her and listen to her as Bill did. Even though she never thought, *If I have an affair with Bill, I'll get Sam's attention on me and off sex and get him to understand what I need from him,* that was what happened.

Insecurity Seeks Validation

Imagine you came to marriage not very sure of yourself. Growing up, you had to perform to get your mother's love or attention. And now your wife doesn't validate you in ways that make you feel adored. It seems sometimes that all you get is a list of things to do or ways she would like you to be different. You go to work, and your female partner thinks you are the best at what you do. In her eyes, you are something else!

Or maybe your wife has never felt that good about herself. When other girls were developing, she was still flat chested, and she never did develop as fully as she wanted to. That has never bothered you, but your words don't seem to make a difference to her. She seemed really turned on to you (seeking your validation) before marriage when you were not sexually active, but now that you are married and having sex, her discomfort with her body gets in the way of her being able to want and enjoy sex with you. What happens when the guy next door expresses his attraction to her?

Addictive Tendencies Hook

Addictive patterns begin during childhood. Being raised in an alcoholic home, with food addictions, abuse, shame, guilt, or rigidity may lead to addictive tendencies. The adrenaline rush of doing something wrong may trigger passion and sexual excitement.

The connection of risk and guilt with sex may have begun with masturbation or getting together with your girlfriend and doing more than you thought was right. When sexual feelings and responses first were elicited in association with an activity that was believed to be wrong, sex may be experienced as feeling good when it's wrong and lack much intensity when it's within the context of marriage where it's considered right.

◆ ◆ ◆

If sex is good only when it's wrong,
it can never be great when it's right.

◆ ◆ ◆

Our finding is that sexual patterns are easily conditioned. The activity or event that evoked sexual feelings and responses for the first time can become the condition that is needed for all future sexual excitement and response. That is one reason we are so adamant that parents teach their children to affirm sexual feelings and take responsibility for their actions. Children must know that God designed their genitals with wonderful sexual feelings and responses and that He designed sexual union and pleasure as an expected part of the marital relationship. Teaching against touching genitals leads to inauthentic guilt and the connection of good God-given sexual feelings with doing wrong. The practice of masturbation will continue, but associated with risk and guilt, not with praise to God and pictures of anticipating marriage. Thus, that individual will come to marriage unable to enjoy the full potential of the pleasure of sex when it is right and be more vulnerable to going for sex when it is wrong!

An Unhappy Marriage Provides an Excuse

No marriage is without some discontent. No spouse can meet all of a person's needs. However, if you fall short on many of Dr. Neil Clark Warren's ten love secrets for a lasting marriage detailed in *The Triumphant Marriage*, if you do not keep your emotional marital bank account full as Gary Smalley talks about in his chapter on marriage in *Go the Distance: The Making of a Promise Keeper*, or if you do not meet the ratio of five positives to one negative that Dr. John Gottman has found as essential to marriages that last (described in *Why Marriages Succeed or Fail*), you are more vulnerable to an affair.

PREVENT AN AFFAIR

Keeping your marriage free of infidelity is a commitment you can master. It will be well worth your effort. Finding intimacy outside marriage may be tempting when life at home gets boring or you feel that you're giving more than you're getting, but not only is it wrong, it's messy.

No One Is Exempt

Face the reality and accept your vulnerability. You may pass the test of vulnerability with flying colors. You may not look to greener grass, be in a situation of possible connection with someone of the opposite sex, face any change or want to effect change in your marriage, be insecure or addictive, and you may be delighted with your relationship with your wife and she with you; you still are not exempt. You are human.

You may have no intention of stirring up feelings with another person. You are not looking for an outside relationship, and neither is your wife. You may not have thought about protecting your marriage from temptation because you never suspected it could happen to you. Beware! No one is exempt from temptation. The Bible is clear that we are to choose one spouse and commit to live faithfully with that spouse for the rest of our lives. It does not say that because we make that choice, we will be free of attraction to others. We are responsive sexual beings, and that responsiveness is not selective. And as the August 15, 1994, *Time* magazine indicates, the current social environment is inhospitable to monogamy (p. 46); nevertheless, we are called to monogamy in our hearts and our actions.

──────── ◆ ◆ ◆ ────────

*Marital love is challenged
when temptation
tests your belief that
love will prevent
an affair.*

──────── ◆ ◆ ◆ ────────

When you are not aware and protecting yourselves and each other, you may be taken by surprise. The feelings for someone else can zap you, or they can build gradually without your realizing how it happened. This chemistry is thought to be brought on by natural aphrodisiacs of the brain. It has nothing to do with love, but the force of infatuation will be far more intense than marital love. And it may challenge your love for each other. This may never happen to you. It may be that once or twice in your lifetime you find yourself suddenly and dramatically attracted to someone. These are the most exciting, but dangerous feelings because they are so powerful and unintentional—almost innocent. Then your belief that your love for each other is sufficient to protect you against such attraction will cause you to question your love.

A Strong Marriage Is a Protective Shield

Sex in America reported an encouraging finding:

Our study clearly shows that no matter how sexually active people are before and between marriages, no matter whether they lived with their sexual partners before marriage or whether they were virgins on their wedding day, marriage is such a powerful social institution that, essentially, married people are nearly all alike—they are faithful to their partner as long as the marriage is intact. . . . Once married, the vast majority have no other sexual partner; their past is essentially erased. Marriage remains the great leveler (p. 105).

Invest Time and Energy

Your marriage will not automatically be a protective shield. You will have to work on your relationship as a couple. Good marriages don't just happen; they take time and energy. Many times a man or woman will complain about a spousal relationship, yet will invest little in improving the marriage. Then when an attraction happens outside the relationship, excessive investment is given to making the new connection work. If that much commitment was put into the marriage, *Hot Monogamy* (the title of a book by therapist Patricia Love) would be inevitable. Invest at least fifteen minutes per day, one evening per week, one day per month, and one weekend per season. This is the Penner formula for a lasting marriage. You will find it throughout the book.

———— ◆ ◆ ◆ ————

Commit: 15 minutes per day
1 evening per week
1 day per month
1 weekend per season

———— ◆ ◆ ◆ ————

We are convinced that if a marriage is going to be more than just functional, it will take time. That time needs to be written into your schedule. Build positive moments. Keep your bank account full with more positives than negatives. If you've encountered a negative, counteract that one negative with five positives.

Understand and Accept Differences

Dr. James Dobson in *Love for a Lifetime* emphasizes that "men and women differ in every cell of their bodies" (p. 43). Even though the feminine uniqueness of your wife likely attracted you to her, probably many times you feel the frustration of Professor Henry Higgins in *My Fair Lady*, "Why can't a woman be more like a man?" Nevertheless, differences can work for you rather than against you when you understand and accept them.

Pursue Common Interests

You and your wife may lose track of common dreams. What did you enjoy doing when you dated? What did you anticipate when you were planning your marriage? What new ideas have you had? Have you listened to her thoughts and goals? Listening does not mean taking action or solving her problems; it only means listening and caring.

Build Togetherness

As sexual therapists, we often get letters and calls from women who are frustrated with their husbands' lack of spiritual and emotional connection with them. They express how much better sex would be for them if they felt their spouses were with them spiritually and emotionally. We recommend these women use their fifteen minutes a day for that purpose. The deal is if you will spend fifteen minutes per day talking, sharing, reading the Bible, and praying with your wife, she'll be more enthusiastic in bed.

Learn to Have Fun and Play Together

Let the child in you play with the child in her. Even though teasing can add a lot of fun, be cautious of teasing. Many children are raised with hurtful or inappropriate teasing that they bring into adulthood and into marriage and hurt each other. Delight in each other. For more ideas see chapter 10.

Renew Your Commitment to Each Other

As 1 Corinthians 13 makes clear, love is not a feeling; it is a commitment to behave lovingly to each other. Love is a precious commodity that increases in value when it is nurtured by the demonstration of respect, tenderness, and thoughtfulness. Love is destroyed and can easily plummet in value when sarcasm, criticism, neglect, and disregard enter any relationship. So regard highly your commitment to love each other by

Never giving up,
Caring more for each other than for self,
Not wanting what you don't have,
Not strutting,
Not having a swelled head,
Not forcing yourself on your wife,
Not always thinking about "me first,"
Not flying off the handle,
Not keeping score of the wrongdoing of your wife,
Not revelling when your wife is groveling,
Taking pleasure in the flowering of the truth,
Putting up with anything, and
Trusting God always (1 Cor. 13, adapted from *The Message*).

A Pure Mind Controls Actions

Philippians 4:8 reads, "Finally, brethren, whatever things are true, whatever things are noble, whatever things are just, whatever things are pure, whatever things are lovely, whatever things are of good report, if there is any virtue and if there is anything praiseworthy—meditate on these things." Your mind has the capacity to think, process, see images, and formulate concepts. The ability to create mental pictures is a wonderful gift. What is put into the mind ultimately affects actions.

You may remember Ted Bundy, the rapist and murderer, who was interviewed by Dr. James Dobson before his execution. He confessed that from a young age he had been exposed to pornography and had filled his mind with more and more violent, distorted input. It was as if that viewpoint became his reality.

Proverbs 23:7 declares, "For as he thinks in his heart, so is he." In psychology, we talk about mental rehearsal. For example, a speaker can rehearse his fear of stumbling when he speaks and be more likely to actually stumble, or he can deal with his fear of stumbling by picturing himself in the speaking situation and performing smoothly. What he rehearses mentally will affect the outcome of his actual presentation.

You, too, can protect yourself against an affair by the images you put into your mind. That does not mean you will not fantasize. You will. That is how your mind has been designed. However, when the fantasies are rehearsed, nurtured, and pursued, they move from imagination to lust, or from a temptation to the sin of committing adultery in your heart (Matt. 5:28). For extra protection, fill your mind with images of loving, fun, fantastic sex with your wife, and free your mind of input that encourages adultery, whether that is pornographic magazines, videos, catalogs, movies, or television programs. Study the positive biblical messages about sexuality. Read the Song of Solomon with your wife.

When Dr. James Dobson coined the phrase *Turn Your Heart Toward Home* for his video series that has been shown throughout the world, he probably did not have this use of that phrase in mind. When feelings of attraction come toward someone who is not your spouse, place your spouse into the picture, and take that new energy and spark home. It works!

A Speedy Exit Will Shortcut Disaster

Flee from temptation. Have a plan of action and live by it. Rehearse your plan mentally. Discuss with your wife what each of you would do if you should find yourself connecting with someone else. When temptation for an affair comes, take prompt, severe action.

1. Tell someone other than the attractee. If your relationship can handle it, tell your spouse.
2. Be accountable to someone other than or in addition to your spouse.
3. Remove yourself from contact with the attractee. That may mean an action as severe as changing jobs.
4. Make a plan to counter temptation should you have accidental contact with the attractee.
5. Rehearse #4 frequently.
6. Stop any fantasies that are rehearsing the temptation.
7. Pour yourself into your marriage, God's Word, and prayer.

Practicing faithfulness in your mind and your actions will bring lasting joy to you as a person and your relationship with your wife. It is worth the effort!

> *Do you know the saying, "Drink from your own rain*
> *barrel,*
> *draw water from your own spring-fed well"?*
> *It's true. Otherwise, you may one day come home*
> *and find your barrel empty and your well polluted*
> (Prov. 5:15, *The Message*).

Chapter 9

Have That Erotic Adventure with Your Wife

If you are looking for some erotic spark in your life, the best place to look is at home.

> **MYTH:** *Sex with the same person over time is no longer passionate or interesting.*

It is true that long-term married sex cannot compete with the grab of a new relationship. However, you may be encouraged to discover, from the findings of the *Sex in America* survey, that monogamous couples are the happiest sexually and are primarily pleased and satisfied with their sexual relationships.

Both Dan and Kate enjoyed their sexual relationship and found they had the qualities of a great marriage. But with both working and their investment in the active lives of their three children, sex wasn't happening as often as they liked.

One day, Dan was meeting with one of his attractive female clients and he found himself imagining pursuing her. He became alarmed, and he thought, *Why not do that with Kate?* That thought began his idea of pursuing his erotic ideas with his wife.

WHY AN EROTIC ADVENTURE?

Something about the hooking nature and newness of an erotic adventure is different from planning a time away. Special times away for a couple are vital to keeping a relationship nurtured, but opening erotic potential with your wife is an adventure only monogamy can bring.

The Adrenaline Hook

Adrenaline is a hormone released in the body in reaction to stress and intense emotions. Stress can be positive or negative. Stress is necessary for us to function, but in excessive amounts, it is destructive. Intense emotions, whether they are manifested as enthusiasm and joy or anger and fear, are the essence of passion. When adrenal hormones are released in response to either stress or intense emotion, most body systems are affected: heart rate increases, breathing changes, male and female hormones react, blood sugar levels elevate, and the total body goes into action to heighten alertness and energy to respond to the stimulus that triggered the adrenaline production.

The revitalizing quality of adrenaline, released in response to powerful emotions, hooks individuals into having an affair. In *The Hidden Link Between Adrenaline and Stress*, Dr. Archibald Hart talks about how so many of us as success-driven Americans are hooked on adrenaline. Adrenaline makes us feel alive and vibrant.

──────── ◆ ◆ ◆ ────────

*The revitalizing quality of adrenaline
is the hook of an affair.*

──────── ◆ ◆ ◆ ────────

To stay alive and vibrant, your marriage needs intensity. Passion will die without expression of a whole range of powerful emotions. The body response is the same to intense love as it is to fear or anger. You may be afraid of your wife's anger, yet you want her to be dynamite in bed. If explosions are going to happen during sex, they are also likely to happen in life. That doesn't mean we give license to destructive expression of anger that can erode a marriage relationship quickly.

◆ ◆ ◆

Passion will die without expression of
a whole range of powerful emotions.

◆ ◆ ◆

You may have to learn to allow yourselves to be vulnerable enough to express the hurts, fears, and frustrations behind your anger and to share your insecurities or jealousies. It is as you are able to express childlike intensity with adult responsibility that you as a couple will connect intensely enough to also feel passion. The emotional bond of opening yourselves with each other without inhibition will keep enough adrenaline coursing through your blood to counteract the "take each other for granted" attitude of a long-term committed relationship.

◆ ◆ ◆

As you are able to express childlike intensity with
adult responsibility, you as a couple will connect
intensely enough to feel passion.

◆ ◆ ◆

Newness

In an affair, everything is new. The two people are new to each other; they discover their bodies, emotions, and intellects. How she looks at him, how he touches her, every interaction is new and exciting. The irritations and disappointments with each other have not surfaced. There are no responsibilities, crises, or burdens to manage. The newness is like the anticipation of an unread novel ready to be discovered.

How can that anticipation and discovery happen between two married people who know each other intimately and have to work to pay the mortgage, unclog the shower drain, take care of their vomiting child in the middle of the night, and try to ignore each other's annoying habits? Creating the newness dimension in your marriage will be more difficult than eliciting a little adrenaline. But you can do it!

A New You

Eliminate your habits that your wife has complained about. If it bugs her when you pick your face, scalp, or nose, STOP! If she has told you she would like you to empathize with her and support her rather than offer solutions when she is emotionally distressed, DO IT! If she has asked you to hang up your clean clothes and put your dirty clothes in the hamper, START NOW! If you used to dress nicely when you were courting her, DO IT FOR HER!

We're working with a couple who are separated and are trying to resolve their issues and get reconnected. They like to bike together, but she is disgusted by how he looks when he bikes. The other day when he was scheduled to meet her to bike with her, he called from his portable telephone to ask her to come out to meet him. She said, "Where are you?" He told her to look across the street. There were a number of bikers. She looked and looked and didn't identify him but then noted a guy in a totally new biking outfit and realized it was her husband. She not only started to laugh but also rushed out to meet him. You may not have a car phone with which to call your wife and you may cause your wife more distress than intrigue and excitement if you buy a new biking outfit, but there are many ways to create a new you. Even small additions or corrections will make a difference.

A New Setting

Where would you have an affair? Take your wife there. It might be a hotel, motel, resort, or your office. Some individuals have walked in on a spouse having an affair in the home, which is a violation of space in addition to the breach of the marital contract and all the accompanying hurt and pain. Your home could be the location of your erotic adventure with your wife, but you would have to invest more time and energy to create a new setting within the familiar space. Whatever location you choose, make it different from what is familiar to the two of you.

A New Experience

It is so natural to repeat the same sexual experience over and over again. Yet if you were with someone new, you would likely be very different with that person. How might you be? What would keep you from behaving that way with your wife? There is so much wasted potential within marriages; there are so many wonderfully new moments to discover. We are sometimes amazed that after more than thirty years of marriage, we find something totally new about one of us that brings a whole new awareness to our enjoyment of each other sexually.

——————— ◆ ◆ ◆ ———————

There is so much wasted potential within marriages; there is so much newness waiting to be discovered.

——————— ◆ ◆ ◆ ———————

You may feel too self-conscious or silly being different or dressing different from your usual self. Nudge yourself a little. If finding a new setting and creating a new experience seem impossible, you might use a book of new ideas. If it is necessary to include her in the fun of planning, that can work, too. Many times erotic adventures evolve through mutual planning of the two interested partners rather than one pursuing the other. Even though you may be reluctant to venture beyond the safe bounds of your current habits, you will experience new vitality with your wife as you strive to capture her heart anew.

HOW DOES AN AFFAIR LOOK?

Having an affair is much more than having sexual intercourse with someone other than a spouse. Usually an emotional, physical, or intellectual attachment binds two people at the expense of their primary relationships. There are risk, secretiveness, planning, presentation of one's best behavior, time commitment, and enticement. The preoccupation brings an affair into the very heart of one's being. These qualities and conditions would be incredibly powerful in any erotic adventure! Practice these conditions with your wife.

Risk

The antidote for losing the passion of a new relationship is the willingness to risk: the willingness to live life with emotional vulnerability and openness, to look for newness, to do the unexpected, to create the conditions of an affair within your marriage.

———— ◆ ◆ ◆ ————

The antidote for losing the passion
of a new relationship is the willingness to risk.

———— ◆ ◆ ◆ ————

Imagine for a moment the risks Dan would have taken had he pursued his client rather than his wife. He would have had to risk letting her know of his attraction to her without knowing of her attraction to him. You can probably fill in your own imagination with ways he might have made the initial move and followed up on his interest in his client with his body language, looks, telephone calls, and eventually action.

Dan let himself do just that with Kate, his wife. He called and talked with her, as he would have pursued his client. He expressed interest in her and what was happening in her day and how impressed he was with how she had handled a project she was working on; he wooed her. At first Kate started questioning his motives, but he kept affirming his positive thoughts and affections toward her. Then he made the hit and invited her to lunch to talk about some decisions they needed to make, which is probably the excuse he would have used to initiate a lunch appointment with his client. Kate felt a sense of curiosity and slight mystique about Dan's approach, but she accepted with somewhat aloof and tingling feelings. That was the beginning of Dan and Kate's revitalizing sexual adventure. Are you willing to make the move on your wife and take the risks that would involve? You might get rejected. Dan might have gotten rejected if he had pursued his client, and he wasn't at all sure that Kate would respond positively. That is the risk that elicited a spark of adrenaline and added a whole new dimension to Dan and Kate's sex life.

Risk occurs in other ways. In addition to the obvious risks of getting caught and the consequences that would place on a person's life, there is the risk of getting to know someone and letting that person get to know you. You may think you know everything about your wife, but many little details are yet to be revealed. Openness to each other brings new discovery and spark in a marriage. As you are willing to get to know each other with a deeper and more intimate awareness—as you are able to be emotionally exposed and naked—you will find that the passion you so desire in your marriage can be resurrected after having been buried for years under layers of assumptions and lack of discovery because you were unwilling to risk letting yourself be known that intimately.

Emotional exposure and nakedness with your wife will spark passion in your marriage.

For most men, the spark of a new relationship is also the energy that gets stimulated in taking the risk of forming an attachment with a woman. That may be more difficult to simulate with your wife since you already feel attached and comfortable with her. You may have to imagine how you won her trust and friendship initially. Winning her anew is likely to stir up romance for both of you. You may feel awkward if you have not behaved in winsome ways with your wife in a long time, but the risk of trying some of those old courting behaviors is the unexpected element that will raise adrenaline levels and vitality.

Secretiveness

The secretiveness of an affair is as energizing as the risk of an affair. Secrets are childlike fantasies enacted in real life. A secret between two people is the cord that ties the two together until the cord is cut when the secret is broken. That is why we recommend that the secret of an attraction outside marriage be shared not with the attractee, but with your wife or someone else.

Creating a secret adventure with the most logical woman in your life, your wife, will get some adrenaline flowing and newness transpiring. It's great for husbands and wives to have secrets—information and experiences they have shared that no one else in the world knows, not even their therapist.

Secrets bind!

Secrets do bind. So why not bind the two of you more tightly and intimately? That may seem scary. Men can be frightened by getting too close and too tightly connected. What if you lose some of yourself or your freedom? That is the risk quality of an affair—of committing yourself to share a secret. But that is also the essence of passion; it is the making of a vital sexual relationship.

Planning

Most affairs are well orchestrated. They are better planned than many dates. There is an obsessive quality in the person pursuing an affair. The anxiety about the risk and the secretiveness increase alertness and repetitive thought processes. That is one of the consequences of the adrenaline reaction. The intensified power competes with the lethargy of an ongoing relationship and leads to detailed anticipation and planning.

You can make beautiful music in your marriage by orchestrating an erotic adventure that has just the right timing, intensity, balance, rhythm, crescendos and decrescendos. You have to know the players; you must know what each of you likes and dislikes and how you respond to various situations and activities. Then you make your plan based on your knowledge of the two of you and your past reactions to past experiences.

When Kate met Dan for lunch, he had the entire afternoon planned for them. He knew Kate would respond positively to a surprise, so he had all the details arranged without her awareness. He had scheduled after-school child care, packed appropriate clothing for both of them, reserved a private booth at a new restaurant, and checked out the hotel room to make certain it had all the accoutrements they would enjoy for their afternoon rendezvous. His planning and anticipation of their likes and dislikes, along with the risk and secretiveness of sneaking away from children and responsibilities, added to their afternoon delight.

Best Behavior

You can count on it that by the time you've invested this much thought and energy in your adventure with your wife, you will be on your best behavior. Certainly, people in affairs bring the best to the affairs, and bringing your best to your time with your wife will enhance the event. It is noteworthy, however, that it takes a special plan to alert you to show your best to the one you love most deeply.

Time Commitment

We are always amazed to discover how much time and energy very busy individuals can invest in an affair. You may be convinced that you cannot take the time to pursue an ongoing erotic relationship with your wife, but we challenge you that if you want the same degree of intensity that you would find in an outside affair, be willing to invest the same time and energy. You will get results.

Enticement

If you find the lively, enthusiastic woman you married to be rather mundane now, you can dazzle her and awaken her sexual vibrancy. Or you may be fortunate to be married to a woman who has not only kept the passion for life and your relationship that she had on your wedding day, but her intensity has continued to blossom and mature. She will become even more alive in response to your enticement.

To lure a woman, you must first clear out past hurts and resentments. You may find it difficult to apologize. It may be even more difficult for you to agree to change your ways to prevent reinjury. But reconciliation is necessary before a woman will respond to a man's enticement.

Your seduction is also likely to elicit a spirited response if your wife feels cared for, understood, and validated by you. You might precede enticement with a check-in talk about how she is feeling about the two of you. John Gray says it well: "When a man loves a woman she begins to shine with love and fulfillment. Most men naively expect that shine to last forever. But to expect her loving nature to be constant is like expecting the weather never to change" (*Men Are from Mars, Women Are from Venus*, p. 113). Make certain you are currently on good terms.

King Solomon in the Song of Solomon is an excellent example of enticement. He adored, praised, and delighted in his wife. She responded by inviting him to enjoy her body. Go for it!

AN AFFAIR SPARKS PASSION

Even though passionate love between lovers is believed to dwindle after the first six to thirty months in a relationship (as reported by Dr. Elaine Hatfield, a psychologist who specializes in research on love), we are convinced that erotic silence is not a necessary consequence of longtime married relationships. Passion may change from the initial newness to deeper fulfillment, but passion is a lifelong possibility.

Passion is not a commodity you were either blessed with or unable to experience. All relationships are capable of passionate intensity. To add the conditions of an affair to the deep love and secure commitment of marriage

is the combination most likely to succeed in developing a lifelong gener-
ous, playful, and mature sexual vibrancy. True passion is being erotic with
someone you know intimately and love and desire so much that you continue to be married to that person. So plan that erotic adventure with your
wife this week.

> *Bless your fresh-flowing fountain!*
> *Enjoy the wife you married as a young man!*
> *Lovely as an angel, beautiful as a rose—*
> *don't ever quit taking delight in her body.*
> *Never take her love for granted!*
> (Prov. 5:18–19, *The Message*).

Chapter 10

Sex: Work or Fun?

Enjoy life with the woman whom you love all the days of your fleeting life which He has given to you under the sun; for this is your reward in life.
—Ecclesiastes 9:9 NASB

Sex is to be fun! The delights of sex are reflected in the pleasure it brings, the charge of the passion, the sensations of the building arousal and the release of an orgasm. The deep satisfaction that comes from connecting at your core with the person you love enough to have committed your life to and the primitive delights of the earthy passion that stirs deep within you are all part of the life-giving and life-perpetuating dimension of sex in marriage.

Sex is also serious and takes work. Spiritually, sex between a husband and a wife symbolizes the most important relationship, the relationship between Christ and His people. Sex reflects the depth of commitment that grows in a relationship. It asks complete abandonment, vulnerability, and release. Serious feelings get stirred up in the process of being sexual. Sexual rights within marriage demand serious respect, and sexual responsibility is a serious requirement of every believer. Sex looms large and weighs heavily when barriers get in the way of all that sex was meant to be.

Sex has to be understood as having both a fun side and a serious side. Sex reflects the light, fun, playful side that the Preacher of Ecclesiastes proclaims as one of the only pleasures of life that a man has the right to enjoy before he dies. And it reflects the serious work side of becoming one, similar to the serious step of becoming one with God, through Christ, by giving all to Him. Work, indeed, is often a prerequisite to fun when it comes to sex in marriage.

SEX WORKS BEST WHEN YOU WORK AT IT: TEN DELIBERATE WAYS

1. Think

The very fact that you're reading this book suggests that you are thinking about sex and have made it a priority in your life. We nudge you to think about what kind of lover you are and how you would like to be. Think through how your sexual life has progressed over the years. What are the messages you have heard from your wife about sex? What sexual tension has there been between the two of you? What is her attitude about your sexual relationship? What are the issues you think about?

You probably plan out your financial future in your mind. You know how you are doing and how you hope to do. You think through your vocational situation and your goals. You think about how you're doing as a parent in raising your children and what you foresee in their future. We suggest you do the same with your sexual life.

2. Plan

Your planning will reflect your thinking. Planning will likely involve bringing your wife into your thinking; planning often becomes a together thing. Your planning might include working on a particular sexual issue, planning a special event or, individually, planning a surprise. Whatever the focus of your planning, your deliberateness will reflect forethought. That forethought will relate to your sexual goals.

You may never have thought of having sexual goals. Goals can be helpful if they are not performance goals that bring pressure and demand. Goals need to be thought of as long-term dreams—ideas that both of you want to work toward over a period of time rather than achievements that you expect to accomplish the next time you're together. They need to be behaviors you can control, not bodily responses that are involuntary.

You may want to work on getting control of premature ejaculation during the next six months. You may want to focus on allowing longer periods of pleasure and increased intensity for your wife (not arousal and orgasm, which are involuntary responses). You may decide you want more atmosphere so you make a plan to take turns preparing the setting for your sexual times. You may plan to read a chapter on sex to each other each week. You may set aside an hour at bedtime several nights a week to just enjoy each other's body with no demand for arousal and release. You may plan how to build a fifteen-minute connecting and kissing time into your daily routine. You may decide to experiment with different methods of birth control that would not be as interruptive as your current method. Make plans to pursue dreams without placing demand or pressure on either of you.

━━━━ ◆ ◆ ◆ ━━━━

Plans need to bring about the fulfillment of mutual dreams, not private dreams that induce pressure or demand.

━━━━ ◆ ◆ ◆ ━━━━

As you plan, set mutual goals that are tangible steps toward enhancing your sexual experience. Whether the planning happens inside you to help you achieve personal sexual goals or between you and your wife, planning without demand will produce positive change.

3. Schedule

Schedule sex? How boring! Think about it. Was dating boring? Did you schedule your dates? Did you become aroused and wish you could have sex?

We remember parking at the conclusion of a scheduled date and kissing and getting so aroused we would drive ourselves and each other crazy with desire to do more. Scheduling increases anticipation, and anticipation sparks passion. You can look forward to your times together and picture how you would like them to be. Try it. You'll like it!

━━━━ ◆ ◆ ◆ ━━━━

Scheduling increases anticipation, and anticipation sparks passion.

━━━━ ◆ ◆ ◆ ━━━━

You may fear that scheduling will take the spontaneity and mystery out of sex. Again, go back to your dating days. Think of the anticipation you felt as you thought about seeing her on Friday night and pictured what you were going to do. You looked forward to feeling her close to you, smelling her perfume, touching her warm hand, holding her, or giving her an extra long, passionate good-night kiss. All of that anticipation led to your excitement in seeing her. Your enthusiasm sparked her. She felt your joy in being with her. The two of you had a wonderful time at a scheduled time. You never said to her, "Oh, we shouldn't schedule to see each other. That would ruin the joy and spontaneity." Rather, having a set time added to your anticipation and joy in being together.

Spontaneity may be great, but it is not a necessary ingredient for an exciting sexual life. Spontaneity works better if led by the woman's desire because the woman's interest can more likely jump-start the man's interest than the man's can the woman's. If spontaneity is going to happen, let it happen by your wife's initiation. That may not seem fair, but it is a reality! Remember the basic principle: A turned-on woman is most often a turn-on to a man, whereas a turned-on man is frequently a demand to a woman. For this reason we emphasize that all spontaneous initiation comes from her unless she ignites in response to your sexual energy.

———— ◆ ◆ ◆ ————

Spontaneity can work if initiated by the woman.
A turned-on woman is usually a turn-on to a man;
a turned-on man is frequently a demand to a woman.

◆ ◆ ◆

———— ◆ ◆ ◆ ————

For most couples, however, scheduling will be necessary. If you don't set aside time to connect sexually, sex won't happen very often, or it will get a few minutes at the most tired end of the day; your physical relationship will get the short shrift. Setting aside times for the two of you on your calendars is absolutely essential to building a quality sexual life.

In your scheduled times, you are not scheduling intercourse, arousal, or release. Just as you did not have them in dating, they are not necessary ingredients to a great and passionate time together in marriage. A common concern is that you should come to your physical or sexual times together already interested or aroused rather than that you could let the feelings grow out of your scheduled time together. It is a myth that the man needs to come to the sexual experience already interested. You're scheduling a time to be together that may or may not grow into a full sexual experience. In contrast to your dating, you now have the freedom to do as much or as little as each of you desires in the moment. You will be amazed at how quickly you can become interested if the two of you spend a little time together and start behaving in sexual ways. You may find that planned time delights your wife because she doesn't feel as hurried or pressured by your new "let's just see what happens" approach.

You may be an exception to our strong recommendation to schedule. If you are together as much as both of you want to be, your sexual life is full and vibrant and mutually satisfying, and you are not scheduling, more power to you. Continue to enjoy and feel fortunate for what you have most naturally.

In spite of their hectic schedules, Sue and Bob always looked forward to their weekly date night.

For the other ninety-nine out of one hundred of you, be like Sue and Bob. Get out your calendars every Sunday night, and make a plan for the week ahead. You can still have spontaneous sex (if she goes for you) at six o'clock in the morning when you wake up or nine o'clock in the evening when the kids happen to go to sleep early. But designing regular times to be together as part of your schedule is essential for most couples.

Also, practice the habit of rescheduling when you cancel a scheduled time. If you are the one who has to cancel, immediately offer another time. For example, if you planned to be together on Wednesday night and you have to stay at the office late or work on a construction site till midnight, call her just as you would have called your date. Let her know that you didn't plan to break the date. Say that you would like the two of you to be together Friday night. Add to the plan by suggesting that you will leave work early and pick her up to have a quick dinner out and then get home by 9:30 so that you can have a couple of hours before the teenagers get home. Rescheduling when you have to cancel is key.

4. Shop

What does shopping have to do with sex? Quite a lot. Shopping with her in mind is one way to tell her you care; it is a tangible demonstration that you are thinking of her. The size of the gift or purchase is insignificant. She doesn't need a new Mercedes to feel that you love her. She needs to know that you planned and thought in anticipation of getting something for her.

Many men fail to notice the tiny needs. If she broke her shoelace for her tennis shoes and you happen to remember to stop and pick up a pair to save her a trip, that $1.49 purchase is of as much value as a new piece of jewelry. It says, "I am thinking about you and wanting to serve you."

Specifically sexual shopping can be fun, too. You may stop at the drugstore and pick up your favorite lubricant, buy scented candles to put by the bed, pick up a rose at the florist on the way home or pick a rose from your garden, get new soft sheets, or buy a book that offers some tantalizing ideas about sex. However, she may consider a book on sex as a message with a demand. If she hasn't read the last three that you bought, you can probably count on her not reading the next one, either. You must also know your wife to know if lingerie would be an appropriate choice. Some wives have enough unused lingerie to open up a lingerie shop. Other wives think of lingerie as for their husbands, so would experience it as a demand. Have a clear understanding of whether she experiences your purchases as pressure and demand or a sign of your thoughtfulness. Sexually oriented purchases are great if they do not put pressure on her.

A fun shopping event is shopping together. You can shop for creams and oils that you both may enjoy or perfumes or articles of clothing for you or her. The shopping agenda must be mutually satisfying.

There are certain shopping requirements. You must remember your anniversary, Valentine's Day, her birthday, Christmas, and Mother's Day (if she is a mother). The gifts for these big events need to represent more than a momentary thought of appreciation. Most men do a pretty good job of the big five. You absolutely cannot use purchases to buy sex or love. Your wife must experience purchases as an outgrowth of your care and thoughtfulness.

◆ ◆ ◆

Shopping can spark sex
if it does not elicit pressure
or attempt to buy sex or love.

◆ ◆ ◆

5. Talk

Men don't want to talk about sex; men want to have sex. Women want to talk about it and have it and talk about it and have it. But primarily, your wife wants to talk; she wants you to be interested in her. You are probably going to have to do the "talk" part if the "have" part is going to be any good. Remember, every time you move in her direction, both of you benefit. You are happier as she is happy; it's a win-win situation.

Talk During Sex

Talking during the sexual experience demands sensitivity. Some couples like to talk a lot during lovemaking while others make love in total silence and are completely happy. Sometimes we encourage couples to experiment with talk during sex. While one pleasures the other, the one being pleasured provides a running commentary on every feeling and thought she has about the touch or her experience. They can repeat the experience with roles reversed. Another option is for the pleasurer to do the talking while enjoying the other's body. Experiment with what works for you.

A woman prefers to have her husband talk about his delight in her rather than her sexual parts. A woman may feel especially depersonalized if these parts are referred to in street language. You may have developed the habit of using explicit sexual talk during lovemaking. Some women love being earthy during sex, yet most find it offensive. Just this week a woman talked to us about how furious she was with her husband for not talking with her about her and for referring to her genitals in slang language as if her sexual parts were her. Sexual talk calls on your sensitivity; your care about her feelings will bring mutual benefit.

Talk during sex about what either of you likes or does not like is often best accompanied by showing. You can plan a show-and-tell time. A demonstration will be a more effective form of communication. When either of you is trying to teach the other about what gives you pleasure, talk about it and demonstrate it at the same time. If you have talked away from the sexual experience about what each likes, then during sex you can refer to that conversation in a few words and with a little bit of touch to communicate what works for both of you.

Talk About Sex

To keep your sexual relationship alive and well, talking very specifically about sex and making decisions about your sexual patterns will need to happen apart from the sexual experience itself. The talk needn't be only about difficulties, challenges, criticisms, and problems; it should also be about what delights each of you and what is especially exciting for you. Share your likes and dislikes.

Talking about sex may seem unnecessary to you. You may assume that because she does not tell you what she likes, you are pleasing her by doing it the way you like. She may be thinking that if you really loved her, you would know what she really liked. So she doesn't tell you that what you're doing bothers her. Her resentment builds while you go on blindly thinking that if she's not saying something, she must be happy.

Apparently I have done something to upset you.

Why is it so hard to talk about sex? Maybe you don't know what words to use. You feel a little embarrassed and awkward because you're not quite sure what to call various parts. You never heard sex talked about in your home. You only heard it talked about crassly on the streets or in the locker room. Street language doesn't seem right to use. To counteract your discomfort, become educated. Read this book aloud with your wife. You will become both knowledgeable and comfortable using correct sexual terminology.

Your hesitancy to open the sexual topic may be your fear of being criticized, of being asked to be or do something that may seem impossible. Or you may fear that you will hurt her if you bring up your true feelings and experience. Criticism about sex is not easy to take. Handling correction, instruction, or criticism is especially difficult when emotions are intense and hearts are wide open with vulnerability. So, plan some talking times about your sexual experience away from the sexual time itself.

Your sexual talk times should have some appropriate boundaries. Neither of you should ever make reference to how some prior partner behaved sexually even if you never had sexual intercourse with that person. The comparisons always end up causing more harm than good. The reasons for making such comparisons are usually hostile. Hostility never serves either spouse.

Another boundary to respect is that you not talk about issues that cannot be changed. Her breast size and her coarse pubic hair are what you got when you married her. Drawing attention to them as troubling issues is the height of folly and can create only tension and distance.

The need for couples to talk about sex became very clear to us years ago when we were doing a two-week series entitled "Pure and Simple Sex" for a television news channel here in Los Angeles. As a part of that show, the producers did a survey of people coming out of divorce court. They asked each couple, "How much did sex have to do with your divorce?" Though the husbands reported that sex had nothing to do with the divorce, the wives reported that it had much to do with it. The lack of awareness of each other's perspective was a clear illustration of how poorly the couple had communicated about their sexual life and how essential it is that talking about sex be an ongoing part of your married life.

6. Learn

Learning about sex is a lifelong process. Parents ask us, "When should we start teaching our children about sex?" We say, "You started at birth, and they will continue to learn until they die." We continue to be amazed at how much we learn about sex and each other sexually after more than thirty years of marriage and twenty years as sexual therapists and educators. We believe that the relationship between God and His people was compared to the sexual relationship in marriage as an indication of never completely knowing. In Ephesians 5, Paul refers to sexual union as the relationship between Christ and the church, a mystery that is forever being revealed but never fully understood. You can still be growing and learning twenty, forty, or sixty years into your marriage. Learning about sex needs a lifelong habit of learning about her and her needs, and about what feels particularly fulfilling and pleasurable to both of you.

Learn About Your Bodies

You need to learn about her body and your body. Talk with each other about body image—how both of you feel about your bodies. Be specific about what you like and don't like about your own body and what each can do to bring your view of your body closer to your ideal. Affirm the positives you feel toward each other's body.

Learn About Your Genitals

Many couples have never looked at each other's genitals or talked about genital touching. Each of you should look at the diagram that labels the parts of your genitals (see pages 35 through 37). Find the various parts. Thank God for each part and the pleasure it brings you. Share that discovery with each other. Pursue teaching each other about or discovering together the kind of genital touch you like. Building familiarity will reduce anxiety and increase pleasure.

Learn About Touching

Teach each other the kind of bodily touching you like. Particularly, learn what she likes, when she likes it, where, how much, how hard, how soft, and everything you can learn about her need for touch. Accept that as her body changes, the wants and desires will change. Her body will go through many more fluctuations than yours because of her monthly cycles, the changes of pregnancy and childbirth, the life cycle of menopause, and perhaps even a hysterectomy. You will have to be forever learning.

An effective way to teach each other about specific touch and stimulation is to guide each other's hands and talk and teach each other what you like. Start with you sitting with your back against the head of the bed and her sitting in front of you with her back to your chest. In that position (or any other position you choose), she puts her hands over yours and guides your hands through an experience of pleasuring and caressing the front of her body (see nondemand position on page 000). When she and you are convinced you clearly understand her likes and dislikes, you reverse roles and you teach her what you like. After guiding her over the top of your body, she can sit between your legs for you to teach her more about genital stimulation of you.

7. Practice

Practicing naturally follows learning. Men seem to have difficulty remembering to practice what they have learned from their wives sexually. You may need to practice ejaculatory control. You may need to practice talking or general caressing or limiting yourself to no genital touch for the first fifteen minutes. You may need continual guidance and practice to stimulate her genitally, either clitorally or intravaginally. Perhaps she responds to G-spot stimulation, which is stimulation of the area in the upper inside of the vagina just beyond the vaginal muscle (see diagram on page 37). You may need a lot of practice finding that area and learning to touch it so that it brings pleasure rather than pain.

Kissing may require both teaching and practice. For some couples, passionate kissing is natural. For many, it is not. Do not assume that she likes the way you kiss. You may be better off to assume that you could learn from her. Let her show you. You will probably like what she likes, but she may not like what you like. Our finding is that when a woman is truly free to teach her husband how she likes to kiss, he loves it. The opposite is often not true. Once she has shown you, spend some time practicing. Even if it's just sixty seconds, take time daily to practice kissing. Kissing is key to keeping sex working!

8. Take Responsibility

Sex works best in a loving relationship if each spouse takes responsibility for himself or herself. Self-stimulation and selfishness are not forms of taking responsibility. Assume that your spouse does not know and cannot sense what feels best to you in any given moment. Even once you have taught each other what you like and each practices the basics, only you will feel what your body hungers for in a specific sexual experience. Learn to listen to and communicate that hunger at the same time that you respond to her communication of what she hungers for.

While you accept mutual responsibility for your sexual desires without demand or violation of the other, you also accept responsibility to enjoy the other's body for your pleasure, counting on the other to let you know if your touch is not pleasurable. The responsibility feedback loop brings the greatest pleasure and enjoyment for both.

The concept of mutual responsibility has radically enhanced couples' sex lives since we first wrote our book *The Gift of Sex* in 1981. This is not a one-sided enjoyment of sex to meet your needs at her expense or you hers at your expense, but an emphasis on both of you taking responsibility, each for yourself with respect and response to the other. This is the most loving way.

9. Negotiate

You can negotiate differences about sex just as you negotiate differences in every other area of life. To be mutually pleasurable and fulfilling, sex must meet both spouses' needs. Sex cannot be dictated by one person.

Whether you want the window open and she wants it closed, whether you want the heat on at night and she wants it off, whether you like fast-food places and she likes slow, leisurely dinners, or whether you like plaids and she likes florals, negotiation is an obvious necessity in every aspect of marriage. Sex is no exception. However, many couples don't think of negotiating about sex. Sex is supposed to click. If it doesn't, couples believe that something is wrong. The truth is that a marriage works best in all areas when a couple learn to negotiate, including negotiating sexual likes and dislikes.

Sex can be worked out so that it benefits both, but sometimes dissimilarities may need to be negotiated. If one of you clearly likes the sexual experience best in the morning and the other likes it best at night, you may find ways to alternate or meet at noon. If one of you loves to make love with bright lights on and all the blankets off the bed and the other prefers the dark and a warm, cozy feeling under the blankets, try dim lighting and less covering. Perhaps one of you really likes oral sex and the other is repulsed by oral stimulation. Respect each other's feelings. The basic rule, however, is to do nothing that is in violation of or at the expense of either individual. In the negotiation process, you always go with the most conservative spouse. That way no one will be violated. Accept that you won't always get what you want.

———— ◆ ◆ ◆ ————

Negotiate your differences
so that both of you are respected and
neither is violated.

———— ◆ ◆ ◆ ————

Following is a checklist of the common differences between spouses. The list reflects personal preferences or discomforts, not rights or wrongs. If either of you considers your preference as the "right way," conflict will be inevitable. Try to respect each other's preferences or discomforts. Each of you should go through and note your responses. Then discuss them. When you agree, you may not need much discussion. If you disagree, you might compare the strength of each response or determine how important that item is to each of you. Since this is not an exhaustive list, you can add your own additional unique differences at the end.

Look at this checklist every year on your anniversary. Use it as a tool to help you accept and negotiate your differences without violating each other. You may want to make copies of this list so each of you has your own list to refer to and to use as a follow-up tool for future reflection.

Common Differences to Be Negotiated

I like to initiate. ___
I like my spouse to initiate. ___

I like making love in the morning. ___
I like making love at night. ___

Direct initiation is the most positive for me. ___
I like subtle initiation. ___

I like to have sex several times per week. ___
Having sex once every week or two is fine for me. ___

Regarding kisses, I like them long ___ and wet ___.
I like kisses to be short ___ and dry ___.

I like to do a lot of talking:
I have little need for talking:

    Before making love. ___
    Before making love. ___

    During making love. ___
    During making love. ___

    After making love. ___
    After making love. ___

I like noisy lovemaking. ___
I like quiet sex. ___

Explicit sexual talk is arousing for me. ___
I like subtle and indirect sexual talk. ___

I like to talk about it afterward. ___
I have no need to talk about it later. ___

I like to get ___ and give ___ lots of touching.
I don't have much need to give ___ or get ___ much touching.

Direct stimulation is most positive for me. ___
I like very indirect stimulation. ___

I like to make love with the lights on. ___

I like the lights off. ___

I like my partner to have eyes open when lovemaking. ___

I am uncomfortable being watched by my spouse in lovemaking. ___

I like oral sex when it is the woman stimulating the man. ___

I don't like oral sex when it is the woman stimulating the man. ___

I like oral sex when it is the man stimulating the woman. ___

I don't like oral sex when it is the man stimulating the woman. ___

I like our lovemaking experiences to be different every time. ___

I like them pretty much the same every time. ___

I look forward to a lot of excitement and creativity. ___

I like predictability. ___

For me there is a strong connection between my sexuality and my spirituality. ___

I am not aware of much connection between my sexuality and my spirituality. ___

Each of you note any of your unique differences that need to be discussed and negotiated.

_____

_____

_____

Walt Nordman was not a morning person.

Doggone it, Margaret. I put that thermostat up there for a reason!

10. Change

Change is constant. The mystery of the gospel and the mystery of sexuality are both unfathomable; growth in understanding and experience is a lifelong expectation for both. You can never expect perfection in either. The calling is to strive toward the mark of the high calling of God and to have a relationship with God that is new every morning. Similarly, you can strive toward deeper love, more intense passion, and closer intimacy with your wife, knowing that you will always be learning and changing and discovering newness together. Change counteracts routine, and since routine stifles passion, change is vital to keeping passion in a marriage.

◆ ◆ ◆

Change counteracts routine;
since routine stifles passion,
change is vital to keeping
passion alive in a marriage.

◆ ◆ ◆

SEX IS MOST FUN WHEN YOU LEARN TO HAVE FUN: TEN DELIBERATE WAYS

1. Laugh

God had quite a sense of humor when He designed sex. Think of getting your bodies together and doing what you do in a sexual experience. When you sit back and think about the uniqueness of the sex act, it's actually hilarious. And to think of the incredibly great feelings that happen in your bodies by doing such rollicking acts.

When sex gets too serious, bring the humorous view of God's design into the bedroom. A little laughter can ease the little mishaps that can get in the way. An elbow in your ribs or a slip of the penis out of the vagina at the wrong moment can be fun if you can laugh together rather than get angry in reaction.

Laughter heals. It can heal hurts, relieve tension, and bring the two of you together. In *Anatomy of an Illness* and *Head First*, Norman Cousins promotes the brain as the largest pharmaceutical house in the world. One of the mediums to tapping the vast healing potential of the human brain is the use of laughter. As you learn to use it, you will find a delightful avenue to sexual joys beyond your cravings.

Silliness can't be planned, but you can allow it and look for opportunities to let it out. We've laughed so hard that several times one of us has fallen off the bed. Once, early in our marriage, we shook the bed with our laughter, and a vase that was on the headboard jiggled off and hit Joyce on the head, giving her a real goose egg. Even though the jolt put a rather immediate end to our laughter, we wondered how we would explain our mishap if Joyce had to go to the emergency room.

Never can laughter berate the other spouse or be at the other's expense. Laughter is fun only if both enjoy it.

2. Experiment

To experiment is to test or try how something works or discover something new. You cannot fail when you experiment because there is no predetermined outcome. When we work with couples in sexual therapy or when couples do the sexual retraining in *Restoring the Pleasure*, they sometimes report discouragement that an exercise "did not work." Our response is that if they tried it, then it worked. Because each assignment is an experiment to learn what each spouse likes, there is no way to fail. There is no prescribed response.

———— ◆ ◆ ◆ ————

You cannot fail when you experiment because there is no predetermined response.

———— ◆ ◆ ◆ ————

You discover new ways of enjoying each other only when you are willing to experiment. Repetition of old patterns provides safety and comfort, but trying a new way sparks new interest and stimulates passion. Yet trying to be experimental may leave you at a loss for ideas. You may believe that you do not have a single creative thought in your brain.

———— ◆ ◆ ◆ ————

Repetition provides safety and comfort; experimentation sparks new interest and stimulates passion.

———— ◆ ◆ ◆ ————

If you are going to try new ways of coming together sexually, you may need a nudge. Your wife may be more of an experimenter than you are. If so, let her lead. Whoever is more likely to risk newness in life will also be the one who wants to push the edge a little bit in the sexual life. If neither of you is apt to be experimental, try some of the following ideas:

- Change who usually initiates.
- Select a new location.
- Take turns being active.
- Start differently from the way you usually do.
- Caress each other everywhere, except don't touch breasts or genitals.
- Use any part of your body except your hands to pleasure your spouse.
- Each choose three objects of different textures to pleasure the other. Start on the other's back and have the one being pleasured guess what is being used and then select one object for a total body caress.
- Act out the breathing and sounds of sexual response.
- Each write a love letter to the other describing a sexual experience of your choice.

- Without entry, try putting your bodies in as may different positions as you can figure out: her on top, you on top, sitting, standing, on the bed, on a chair, side by side, legs between, legs around, on the edge of the bed, kneeling beside the bed, spooning (one behind the other), etc. You can have fun experimenting with how your bodies fit together and work best. Without any stimulating or arousal, getting into positions to see how they would work will certainly add some silliness, and you may even find something that you like.

3. Surprise

Surprises thrill some people and immobilize others. If you or your wife is affected negatively by being surprised, you need to know that about each other and respect your unique qualities. If surprises are not negative for the other spouse, a little surprising action or gesture can clearly send the message of thoughtfulness.

For the spouse who prefers predictability, plan your surprises together. Plan her surprise birthday party with her. Give her the gifts from her gift list. Decide together on a special evening or sexual time. If you do initiate a surprise, make it a small expression that demands no response. Usually, the person who is immobilized by surprises has to integrate the data before being able to respond. The benefit of the surprise is lost in the scramble to come up with the appropriate response. A surprise feels too demanding to that person.

———— ◆ ◆ ◆ ————

*When surprises immobilize,
plan surprises together.*

———— ◆ ◆ ◆ ————

On the other hand, if your wife experiences surprises as a language of love and you do surprises well, go for it. Sexual surprises will add a lot of fun for the two of you. You might pack an accoutrement such as a feather in the luggage to pleasure her with when you arrive at the hotel. You might have a surprise gift that you pull out from under the bedcovers. You might show up early from work with dinner on an evening when you know she is stressed and has been missing you. When she gets home from work late, you might have a bubble bath run for her, have the children in bed, and have a lotion warmed and ready to caress her without any expectation that she respond with arousal, release, or desire for intercourse. Most women prefer tender, loving, thoughtful surprises rather than the kind of surprises that have too much adrenaline connected with them. All surprises must be freely given without a demand for response.

Surprises involve some risk. Not every surprise is going to work, but as you are willing to risk, you will discover what does work.

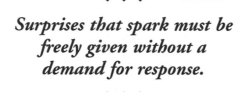

Surprises that spark must be freely given without a demand for response.

4. Shock

A shock is a BIG surprise. When we were taping our video series *The Magic and Mystery of Sex* in Cleveland, we asked one couple, John and Becky, what kept their sexual life so vibrant. Becky replied, "A bit of a shock every now and then." Cliff asked, "Oh, you mean when you meet him at the door in Saran Wrap?" She laughingly indicated that it was when he met her at the door in Saran Wrap. He was the house dad at the time, and she was working outside the home. A little shock, a slight shake-up, or a new burst of interest, excitement, or adrenaline is a source of energy to get you connected with each other and bring passion.

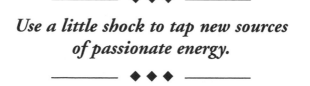

Use a little shock to tap new sources of passionate energy.

5. Treat

Treats are endless resources of sexual fun. A woman who is able to receive loves being treated. Treat her to rose petals spread on the sheets when she crawls into bed, a love nest in front of the fireplace, an hour of your undivided attention, an evening to sit and read while you tend the children, a body caress, or time that is focused completely on what she wants.

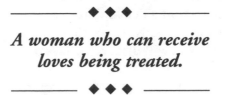

A woman who can receive loves being treated.

Treats that spark sexual passion for a woman do not tend to be the pornographic type promoted in men's magazines or on late night television. We encourage ordinary treats that ordinary couples can enjoy together. The treats we recommend fall into these main categories: purchases, accoutrements, preparation, attention, and activities.

Purchases, as we mentioned in our suggestions for shopping, do not require using up the family inheritance; little gifts can show your forethought. Remember, a woman appreciates the thought as much as she does the size of the gift. You might buy food that the two of you enjoy sharing, music that has some positive memory connected with it, clothing for her that she has been wanting or makes her attractive to you, or clothing for you that you know would increase your attractiveness to her. The purchase of a gift or a card with a warm communicating message is a way of treating and showing that you care.

Did you remember the mousse?

Accoutrements are little extras that send the message of love and can have a powerful impact on the woman. Think of the treat of staying at a nice hotel and having your bed turned down and a chocolate mint or flower on your pillow when you return to your room at the end of an evening. It gives you a feeling of specialness. It didn't take long, it didn't cost much money, but it makes you feel special. Accoutrements can be extras that add to the setting, such as candles lit when she comes from the bathroom, a flower at the bedside, or items to use during sexual pleasuring, such as warm oils or a feather or an item of satin. Accoutrements tend to be sensuous treats that can be customary or more exotic.

Preparation shows love and forethought by taking time to prepare yourself, the atmosphere, or some other aspect for the two of you coming together: lighting a fireplace, heating or cooling the room, adjusting the lighting, setting the music, showering, shaving, putting on cologne, cleaning up your mess in the bedroom, organizing the evening for the two of you to have time to connect. Preparation can be a strong message of love.

Attention may be the biggest winner with your wife. Turn off the television and the computer. Your attention to her on her terms could be the treat of the century. Try it!

Activities that women consider treats vary from woman to woman. You need to know the woman you've married. She may like it if you join her in the bubble bath or shower, she may prefer a dinner out before lovemaking, she may love dancing together, or she may enjoy specific sexual activities. Maybe she would love an evening of sitting on the couch, talking, kissing passionately, and making out. You can initiate a variety of activities that would be treats for both of you.

6. Pleasure

Our good friend Roland says, "Why do you guys always talk about pleasuring?" It's true—Penners promote pleasure. If you've read any of our books, including what you have read in this one, you know that pleasure is central to our message about sex in marriage. You can never go wrong if you focus on pleasure. If both of you are taking responsibility for doing what feels good to you and respecting what feels good to the other, the giving and receiving of pleasure is guaranteed not to fail.

———— ◆ ◆ ◆ ————

The giving and receiving of pleasure is guaranteed not to fail.

———— ◆ ◆ ◆ ————

Pleasure or pleasuring refers to skin-to-skin touch that has no demand for arousal or orgasm or any response or action. It is just for the sake of touching and being touched. No demand means exactly that. There is no expectation; your and her responses to the touch can be pleasant, warm, comfortable, enjoyable, arousing, or neutral. The pleasuring can be an end in itself, or it can lead to an erotic lovemaking experience.

The time you take to pleasure and the extent of bodily involvement can vary. Even five minutes will build positive connection. A more extended time can focus on the whole body. Sometimes you may enjoy giving each other a foot caress. You may be unaware of how sensuous the feet are, especially your wife's. Jesus washed His disciples' feet, not for the sake of sexual pleasure, but to demonstrate servanthood and intimacy. As you lovingly caress your wife's feet, hands, face, back, or whole body, you send a message of love and honor for her personhood. When your focus is not on her breasts and genitals for the purpose of stimulation, she will feel honored and adored by you. Then she will open her soul to you.

Enjoying the pleasure of each other's body can be expressed through many forms. You may try one of the experimental ideas we suggested earlier. Use any part of your body, other than your hands to pleasure each other. Your hair, your nose, your forearms, or even your toes can be used to stretch the sensuous awareness of your bodies. Perhaps you would enjoy combing or brushing each other's hair. Some people love that. Cliff dislikes his hair being touched, but he can always count on Joyce relaxing if he strokes her hair. You might choose various textured objects to pleasure each other and try to guess what object the other has chosen. Silk or satin will feel very different from feathers or tissue or a roller brush. Cuddling is another form of giving and receiving pleasure. Lying next to each other in each other's arms, feeling each other's body, may build closeness that leads to more intense passion or just meshing and relaxation. The cuddling can be with clothes on, in nightclothes, or in the nude. Have fun with each other through the giving and receiving of touch.

Taking turns with pleasuring, that is, alternating which one of you is doing the touching and which is receiving the touching, will give each of you an opportunity to enjoy the sensation of your own body being touched and touching the other's body. This is what we mean by soaking in. You start by receiving the touch on the outside and then let the touch reach the inner part of your being.

7. Tease

Teasing can be fun, or it can sting. Each spouse comes with a unique history and response to teasing and being teased. Thus, you have to be sensitive to the other person and take responsibility to let the other know your limits for teasing.

Teasing can take many forms. In chapter 3, we recommended teasing touch as an approach to keep your wife hungry for more touch and to let her lead in the sexual experience. Tickling can be a form of teasing that some couples enjoy. Verbal teasing includes a bit of razzing and poking fun at yourselves or each other. Verbal teases can quickly cross the line from fun to irritation or hurt. Teases that are passive expressions of anger have no place in lovemaking. Keep all teasing fun and light and free of personal jabs.

Just as teasing touch can be a form of the man letting the woman lead, tickles and teasing touch can also be tools to distract from performance anxieties or demands. In the sexual experience, when you sense the touching is moving from a focus on pleasure to an expectation of arousal, you can incorporate the teasing touch of chapter 3. Rather than perpetuating demand for response by going for her genitals and trying to get them to respond, back off.

Kissing can be incorporated in the enjoyment of your teasing by varying the degree of light kissing to more passionate involvement. The important guideline is to always lighten up before it gets to be too much for her. Remember with a woman, it is always better to have her hungry for more than for her to feel that she is being smothered, bombarded, or overwhelmed. Wait until she either takes your hand or moves her body or begs for more direct stimulation. As Solomon experienced with his new bride, you want her to say, "Quit fooling around 'cause my body can't stand it anymore. I'm getting so hungry for more that my body is dripping." Rather than feeling pressure to respond, she becomes hungry to respond.

———————— ◆ ◆ ◆ ————————

It is always better to keep a woman
hungry for more than to
smother, bombard, or overwhelm her.

◆ ◆ ◆

———————— ◆ ◆ ◆ ————————

8. Resist

Playful resisting can be great fun. When you sense you've moved in on her a little too eagerly, quickly switch to playing hard to get. You both know she can get you in a second if she really wants to, but your playful resistance will function as a positive lure to her. You may pretend to be asleep, claim you have a headache, or say you're not really interested tonight after all. Indeed, you are just setting her up to come after you. The silliness can be another distraction from your tendency to push for more too quickly.

9. Create

Creative additions to sex have a way of sparking interest, heightening arousal, building intensity, and communicating a message of love and care that is qualitatively different from doing the same old thing. Create your own special setting. One couple turned their mobile home that was set up for pickling and canning vegetables in summer into their retreat from their children. Another couple made a love nest in her sewing room. Another man invited his wife to his office where he had a special romantic dinner brought in and served. You may have a van or pickup camper that you can use for romping, a secluded area on your patio, a guest bedroom, or a comforter on the floor anywhere that is private.

Creativity can happen in your natural context regardless of your circumstances. You do not have to invest money or a lot of time. Some forethought will usually be necessary. Your creations could be additions to the lovemaking event itself. You might switch roles or create new ways of sharing and enjoying each other's bodies. Your creativity can be costly and elegant or humble and plain and yet be the addition that communicates the message of attentiveness that your wife will love.

The summer after we were married, we worked as interim pastors for a small church in central Canada, and we lived in a home that had one tiny bed, one table, and two chairs. We carried our water down the street and used the outdoor "biffy." Yet we found ways to turn our austere situation into fun rather than despair. We found that a creaky, wire spring bed can add pleasure when used correctly! With no money and the promise of not much more to come, we had fun, exciting times together.

10. Play

Playing at sex is the most fun of all. Play house, play doctor, play dress up, play "I'll show you mine if you'll show me yours," play charades, act out the Song of Solomon, or choose your own form of play. Pretending that is not deceiving each other can be your form of play. Take on the role of a personality on television or in a favorite movie. Act out the breathing and sounds of sexual arousal and release. You will probably spend most of your time laughing while you are pretending. It can be a hilarious time together. Whether your play is preplanned or in the moment, learn to have fun by playing together during sex.

USE ALL SEVEN OF YOUR SENSES

You know the five senses. Dr. Stella Resnick wrote about a sixth sense, the inner sense, in the July 1988 edition of *Self* magazine (pp. 98–103). We have added a seventh sense, your empathetic sense. All seven of these senses will affect the sexual experience for you and for your wife. These senses are sensual gates to sexuality. You can use one gate or many gates to bring your total person—heart, soul, mind, and being—to the sexual experience and engage her total person of heart, soul, mind, and being. As you connect all of you with all of her through the seven senses, you move the two of you to a greater, more passionate, more intimate, and more intense sexual life together.

1. Seeing

Men are known to be visual responders. You know what triggers you sexually. You may have to be careful to control what or who you look at so that your sexual responsiveness is not solicited outside your marriage and is nurtured within your marriage.

Kent, one of the men Harold Smith interviewed for *Marriage Partnership*, expressed his need to keep his visual responsiveness in control:

In our culture, discipline and sex seem at cross-purposes. But without discipline, I'm convinced you can't have a good marital sex life. Without discipline, you're free to focus on any and everybody, sexually speaking—not just your wife.

Sexual discipline calls for an almost legalistic mindset: "I will not look at that R-rated video" or "I will not go out to lunch with a woman alone." Such a legalism is not based so much on paranoia as it is on keeping your marriage—and marital sex—free from the encumbrances of unrealistic expectations and fantasies (*Marriage Partnership*, Winter 1993, p. 50).

A man may get aroused at the very sight of his wife in some state of undress or in seductive clothes. You can use your instant responsiveness to your wife to build your sexual relationship or shut it down. If your response to her puts you into action, she will learn to dress cautiously and not change clothes in front of you. Her caution will decrease her sexuality and take away from your pleasure. On the other hand, if you use your responsiveness to honor her with your praise and enjoyment without action, she will invite you into her sexual world and build her enjoyment of her sexuality.

Women do not tend to respond in the same visual manner as do men. Yes, it is important for you to look attractive and take care of yourself, but that is just a gate to respect that might lead to sexual interest later. The visual is more of a necessity for the relationship than a direct turn-on. If you walked into the room to find your wife lying on the bed in a provocative pose, wearing something sexually enticing, you would probably hope to ravish her body. Whereas if you were to lie on the bed with an erection and wait for her, your wife would probably be put off by the demand that she would feel. Yet many men have the idea that somehow the aroused man is a draw to the woman. When the woman is interested or aroused, she will enjoy the man's sexuality, but for most women, the man's arousal is not a starting point.

Men and women often respond to an erection as a requirement for ejaculation. When an erection communicates such a demand, it is a negative visual stimulus for the woman. On the contrary, if you recognize that your erection is an involuntary response that can come and go without the need to pursue ejaculation or intercourse, your wife will be more likely to view your erection as user-friendly. You started having erections within minutes after you were born and have one every eighty to ninety minutes while you sleep. So erections are a very natural ebb and flow of life.

Both of you can learn to use your visual gate to enhance your sexual experiences. Keeping your eyes open before lovemaking and during sex builds intimacy and intensity. Enjoyment and appreciation of each other are enhanced. Your responses will play off each other and have an escalating effect on your erotic enjoyment. If both are used to having your eyes closed, try keeping them open a little at a time. It can be one more fun ingredient of your sexual times.

2. Smelling

Chemistry between lovers may be based primarily on smell. You may have read about research on pheromones, the sexual scents animals give off at mating time. The current suspicion is that human beings emit odors that attract or distract selective members of the opposite sex. Each of you may send off scents that invite the sexuality of the other or repel closeness.

The positive smells from body lotion, perfume, and aftershave tend to enhance sexual attractiveness, at least in our culture. Perfumes react differently on different skin. A fun treat for the two of you would be to visit a department store and try different scents to evaluate which types you like on each other.

Natural body odors of arousal, perspiration, and sexual secretions also have the capacity to elicit attraction. The importance of these and their arousal capability vary from culture to culture and time to time. Travelers are often amazed that the smells of the residents of the culture they are visiting are acceptable in that culture. In times past, the musky odors of not bathing were experienced as a sexual invitation for a man. Napoleon is known to have written home to his wife not to bathe because he was coming home. You would probably write the exact opposite.

Odors are sensitive issues for sexual functioning. Breath, body, hair, genitals, and feet can be a source of repulsion from one spouse to another. If you are going to honor your wife, you will be attentive to caring for your body and respecting her needs for cleanliness and smells. You will also need to be sensitive in communicating to her if there are issues with her odors that offend you. A talk away from the bedroom and a sexual time will be the best way to deal with odors. There is no way to expect your wife to be responsive if you haven't taken care of your body. And she, generally speaking, is the best judge of whether or not you have cared for it. Her love for you is not enough to cover bad smells. Honor your wife by hearing and taking seriously any body or odor issues for the rest of your life.

3. Touching

The touching sense is about enjoying pleasure without demand for response. It is the primary sense used during sex. Every square centimeter of your body has thousands of receptors that take in and transmit the touch to the brain, and then emit sensations throughout your entire being. A woman may feel loved when she is touched with a light butterfly touch, a whispery touch, tickles, or a warm, firm touch. A man receives pleasure when he touches certain curves in a woman's body. The woman's waist, the shape of her legs, her feet, the silkiness of her skin, or the contours of her breasts, all have sensations of enjoyment.

The man's enjoyment of the woman's body can be a beautiful experience or one of tension. Conflict about his enjoyment of her usually occurs when the man assumes his right to the woman's body and is not willing to let her be the authority on how she wants to be touched. He touches the way he would like to be touched instead of letting her be the authority on her body and touching her the way she desires.

If you are looking for change in your sexual life, the very next time you're together let her guide you or start by having her describe exactly how she would like to be touched. If she is unwilling or unable to tell you or guide you, change how you touch by lightening your touch by at least a half, and do not increase the firmness until she invites it. Keep your touch general until she wants it to be more specific. We almost guarantee that within the first week or two, your wife will notice and reinforce your new way of touching.

4. Tasting

The tastes of sex are mainly subtle. Feeding each other or enjoying eating together can add sensuousness to your sexual experience. Most of the tastes of sex, however, will be experienced as lips and tongue happen to land on each other's body and mouth. The wonderful miracle of kissing will be your most used avenue of sensuous tasting. Kissing is the most personal, the most intimate, part of the sexual experience, even more personal than getting genitals together. You give yourself to your wife when you passionately kiss her.

Kissing and tasting each other's total body can be another avenue of opening yourselves to each other. The tastes are one of a kind and represent your particular relationship and probably part of what draws you to each other. The Song of Solomon is a beautiful, symbolic description of a bride and a bridegroom licking, tasting, eating, and drinking of each other's sexual secretions: "Let my beloved come to his garden and eat its pleasant fruits" (4:16). King Solomon says, "I have come to my garden. . . . I have eaten my honeycomb with my honey" (5:1). The lovers of the Song of Solomon refer to the genitals as the garden of spices. Using the mouth to enjoy the other's genitals has been a topic of controversy for generations. Sensitivity and respect for each of your areas of caution and possible violation are necessary.

Each of you will be keenly aware and affected by how the other tastes. Keep yourselves clean for each other, and respect each other's boundaries.

5. Hearing

The sense of hearing is primarily used to communicate or express sexual pleasure. During sex, the ears take in words of expression, noises of responsiveness, and background sounds that you have provided.

We hope your words of expression are words of adoration, love, delight, and appreciation that you share in the throes of lovemaking. Words of invitation enhance; words of correction or criticism distract and hurt. Words during sexual intimacy must be carefully chosen.

The noises of your bodies and your voices communicate the excitement of the moment and the level of intensity that you're experiencing. The involuntary expressions have the effect of bringing even more arousal. If you are a silent lover, take heed. The gasps, moans, groans, grunts, and deep breathing of the natural sexual response are sexual music to the ears of your lover and bring great joy. If you have never learned to let out your sexual intensity, practice the breathing and sounds of a sexual experience at some separate time. You can have a lot of fun mimicking each other.

Providing background sound can be another sensuous addition. You may like music or a tape of ocean waves or of a rainfall. The two of you can have fun listening to a variety of background possibilities to find ones that you both agree would be fun to have on during your sexual times. Background sounds can also provide a sound barrier to protect you from others' noises and others from you.

6. Inner Sensing

Attending to your inner sense and enhancing your wife's ability to attend to her inner sense will change your sexual experience from a superficial expression to a much deeper sharing of who each is. Your inner sensing will lead you to attending to what's going on in your brain, your genitals, your skin, your body, your fantasies, your breathing, and all of your other senses. Put all your inner attending together in a blender and you have that inner sense. Your inner sense is your integration sense. It is greater than just the sum of the individual parts; it is the sense that gives you the capacity for your sexual response.

7. Empathetic Sensing

The Random House Dictionary of the English Language, the Unabridged Edition (1967) states that "empathy is more enduring and valuable than romantic love" (p. 468). The sense of being able to connect with the feelings, thoughts, and desires of the one you love is the talent of a man who has promised himself to his wife to love for his lifetime.

At the same time that you are attending to your inner sense, you are respecting and responding to your wife's signals and your sense of what is going on in her body. You get with her inner sense. You are listening to her and allowing her to pursue pleasure for herself. You are connecting with her thoughts and feelings as she is able to take responsibility to know herself and share herself with you. Empathy is not guessing what she wants and behaving as if you are the authority on her desires, but attending to the sense of herself that she shares with you.

Your empathetic sense, the seventh sense, brings you and your wife together in the powerful, mystical union of "becoming one flesh." Sexual union with empathetic sensing is truly becoming one flesh, one spirit, and one mind. A husband and a wife, each in tune with the inner sense, for those moments fuse their two inner senses into one. That fusion makes sex in marriage powerfully erotic, intense, spiritual, and overwhelming. When this mystical union takes place, it is a power that transcends all of the rest of life like the mystical union that occurs when God enters the life of a person on this earth and transforms that life.

◆ ◆ ◆

When a husband and a wife, each in tune with the inner sense, empathetically become one, the power of that union is like the mystical union of God entering a human life.

◆ ◆ ◆

USE YOUR MIND

The brain is the biggest and most powerful sex organ. The brain manages all of sexual functioning through the chemicals it secretes, the nervous system it regulates, and the muscles it controls. In addition to managing sexual functioning, it is the house of all mental images.

Your mind can create what you choose. Reality is not a necessity for mental images. The ability to create mental pictures in your mind is called fantasy. It is part of your having been created in God's image different from the rest of the animal kingdom. You can think, feel, imagine, and project.

Images will also involuntarily drift across your mind, even when you haven't chosen them. These passing images will be influenced by what you put into your mind, by what you see on television or in the movies, what you read in books, hear in songs, or have experienced. But images can also come across your mind that seem to have no obvious or apparent conscious source in your recent or even distant experience. All images are fantasies or imaginations.

As we noted in chapter 8, you are responsible for what you choose to put into your mind and for what you do with the images that involuntarily enter your mind. You can choose to nurture and build positive images, and you can stop negative images. The New Testament teaches that since through Christ believers are freed from the law, all things are possible for those who love God and are called according to His purpose, but not all things are edifying. The responsibility of the believer is to put pictures into the mind that edify the marriage and the relationship with God.

— ◆ ◆ ◆ —

KEY CONCEPT:
The capacity for fantasizing is God-given;
the responsibility for the content of the fantasy
is personal.

— ◆ ◆ ◆ —

The key concept is that the capacity for fantasizing is God-given; the responsibility for the content of the fantasy is personal. God designed you as a sexually responsive person. Your responsiveness is not selective, but you are called by God to take responsibility to be selective in what you pursue both in your mind and in your actions. In many ways this is no different from any other area of life. God gave humankind the freedom of choice. Just as you are called to be responsible for choices in relation to your body and your resources, you are also responsible for the use of your fantasies.

Sexual intimacy and fulfillment were designed for marriage. Anything of the heart or the mind or an action that distorts that union or distracts from it, Christ says will turn fantasy to lust and lust to adultery (Matt. 5:28). For this reason, we continue to encourage you to put the face of your beloved in place of any picture, image, or temptation that enters your mind. Always turn your mind toward home!

Fantasy will build your marital relationship when you use it to create with your wife dreams of mutual enjoyment and pleasure. You don't have to own a home on the beach or in the desert or sail the ocean romantically together. You can experience any reality you choose to generate in your mind. Joseph Dillow, in *Solomon on Sex*, says, "I think it's time we Christian brothers used some sanctified imagination around our home" (p. 24). Use your mind to be creative, expressive, poetic, enticing, seductive, and intimate with your wife.

> *And I have seen that nothing is better*
> *than that man should be happy in his*
> *activities, for that is his lot*
> (Eccl. 3:22 NASB).

Chapter 11

A Word to the Wives Is Sufficient

Wife, you, too, can discover greater love, passion, and intimacy in your marriage. You may have read his chapters, which we encourage. However, they *are for him*. And, husband, this chapter *is for her*. You can read hers, but you absolutely cannot make one comment about her doing her part, and she cannot make a comment about you doing your work. Each of you is responsible for your attitude and approach to making your sexual life more fulfilling. You are not responsible for what the other is to do or be. That is a boundary you must respect to effectively apply the sexual ideal we are promoting.

In the introduction to this book, we define the ideal that we believe will bring greater love, passion, and intimacy to sex in marriage. The ideal is for mutual sexual joy and fulfillment. That ideal can be attained only when each spouse takes responsibility to do his or her part and releases responsibility to the other for his or her part. The key concept is that as your husband loves, honors, and serves you, his affirmation will allow you to open yourself to enjoy mutual sexual pleasure with him.

◆ ◆ ◆

Mutual sexual joy and fulfillment
can be attained only as each spouse
takes responsibility to do his or her part and
releases responsibility to the other
for his or her part.

◆ ◆ ◆

◆ ◆ ◆

KEY CONCEPT:
As your husband loves, honors, and serves
you, his affirmation will allow
you to open yourself to enjoy mutual sexual
pleasure with him.

◆ ◆ ◆

What is your part? The woman best serves the man by allowing herself to be aware of her sexuality and to share it openly with him. Remember, nothing turns on a man more than a turned-on woman. And as you are able to discover and know yourself and share yourself freely and openly with him, he will feel served. Your roles of giving yourselves to each other sexually are different.

◆ ◆ ◆

The woman serves the man by getting
with all of her sexuality for herself
and then sharing it with him.

◆ ◆ ◆

Each chapter concept that addressed him has a companion side for you. As you apply these following complementary concepts and he applies the concepts he has learned in the previous chapters, you will discover greater love, passion, and intimacy in your marriage.

ENJOY THE PROCESS

Just as men like results, women like the process. Men tend to approach sex to score; they are goal oriented. Women are more likely to approach sex to enjoy the closeness and connection. Women prefer to cuddle; men prefer to just have sex. Go with your likes; sex for both of you will be better when both enjoy the process.

When a woman joins a man in a goal-oriented approach to sex, sex is great initially, but the spark dies quickly. Your mother or society may have trained you to think of sex as primarily for the man. They were wrong!

If you don't think of sex for you, you come with goals similar to his. You may believe that you should be interested anytime he is interested or that you should be able to get aroused when he goes straight for your sexual buttons. You may be convinced that you need to focus on pleasing him, so you have relinquished focusing on your pleasure. You may have no idea what your body would enjoy. Maybe you believe that you should get quickly aroused and have an orgasm or half a dozen orgasms. When he gets upset because you don't have an orgasm during intercourse, you become convinced that you should. You may have lost interest in sex because you have felt like a failure in achieving the goals that you thought were important to satisfy him and have a happy sex life. Whatever the demands you have placed on yourself or him, goal-oriented sex will not work any better for you than it does for him.

◆ ◆ ◆

Goal-oriented sex won't work any better for you than it does for him.

◆ ◆ ◆

Sex is about the process of enjoying pleasure, not about your pleasing him or his pleasing you. Mutual pleasure is the refrain of sexual fulfillment. Ultimately, your husband will be pleased only when you are pleased, and you will be pleased only when you respond to your natural instincts of extending and enjoying pleasure. When you listen to and pursue your needs for pleasure, you will be totally satisfied. Then he, too, will be satisfied. Hence, you serve him most by pursuing your sexuality and making sure you are pleased.

◆ ◆ ◆

Sex is about enjoying mutual pleasure, not about your pleasing him or his pleasing you.

◆ ◆ ◆

Focus on pleasure rather than on stimulation. Let the stimulation be the by-product if it happens. If it doesn't, you have had a good time and made a warm connection; that is the most important goal.

Some women equate being pleasured with being aroused. They report that an assigned pleasuring exercise didn't work for them because they didn't get any pleasure from it. They mean they didn't get aroused. They will not want to do the clinical genital exam to teach what genital touching they like because they think unless the touching produces arousal, it has not been pleasurable or beneficial.

The only criterion for receiving pleasure is that the touch does not feel irritating or painful or negative in any way. Think of the sensation of your husband's touch on a scale of zero to ten. If zero is neutral and ten produces an orgasm, as long as the touch is zero or above, you are receiving pleasure. Zero is just fine.

◆ ◆ ◆

The criterion for pleasure is that the touch is not negative; arousal is not necessary for pleasure.

◆ ◆ ◆

You may enjoy being stimulated and experience the responses of arousal and release. Desire for the enjoyment of arousal and release is normal, but it cannot be the goal; it must be the consequence of greater and greater levels of longer and longer times of pleasure. You have to lose your life to gain it; you must abandon goals of arousal and release to allow the involuntary reflex responses to happen.

◆ ◆ ◆

Redefine your goal to go for higher levels and longer times of pleasure rather than for arousal and release.

◆ ◆ ◆

You can compare the "lose your life to gain it" approach to many other pursuits of life. If a musician strains to hit a high or low note, it won't work because she is trying too hard. If she lets it flow from deep inside her, she will be able to open up and let the beautiful notes resonate out. The same is true in sex. An athlete is much more likely to reach her potential if she prepares her body through diligent training and then loses herself in the activity of her sport, reducing the stridency, rather than straining to reach her goal. Exactly the same thing is true in your sexual life.

As you are able to let go and focus on the pleasure of the sexual experience, you will find the greatest excitement, arousal, and ecstasy. When you are not goal oriented or watching your response, you will allow the natural intensity to develop that is possible when you are focused on the pleasure of the sensation of the touch.

———— ◆ ◆ ◆ ————

As you are able to let go
and focus on the pleasure,
you will discover the greatest excitement,
arousal, and ecstasy.

———— ◆ ◆ ◆ ————

LISTEN TO YOUR BODY

Good sex doesn't just happen, but you can make it happen by listening to your body. You can't use any external authority as the final authority about you and your body and your sexual response. You are the only authority on what your body needs and wants.

———— ◆ ◆ ◆ ————

You can make good sex happen
by listening to your body;
you are the only authority
on what your body needs and wants.

———— ◆ ◆ ◆ ————

Society Is Not Your Authority

Society can try to assume authority on your sexuality by saying, "Just do what comes naturally." We hope you have no live model of how to have sex naturally, so how would you know? If you have observed sex in movies and on television, it was likely sex outside marriage. That irresistible type of sex driven by pure passion doesn't happen very often in marriage. So, you're probably not doing naturally in your marriage what you saw in the movies. You are not likely to have a very good sense of what is natural.

Magazines Are Not Your Authority

Women's magazines have articles on helping you be a better, more passionate sexual partner. You may glean helpful suggestions, but the articles cannot be your final authority. The information may not concur with your moral stance. The sexual techniques and approach may be radically different from what you enjoy. The national averages or findings on women may give you a perspective of where you are in relation to other women, but the statistics are not authoritative statements of what you should like or not like. You do not have to live up to the findings on other women. What is essential is that you learn to go inside yourself and listen to what your body is telling you, what your spirit is telling you. You are your own best authority.

◆ ◆ ◆

Learn to go inside yourself;
listen to what your body and your spirit
are telling you.

◆ ◆ ◆

Medical Doctors Are Not Your Authority

Your medical doctor has technical knowledge that will help you with hormonal levels or infections or other bodily functions that affect your sexual experience. But even he or she is not the final authority on your sexuality or your body. Your doctor may say, "Go home and do this and you'll be just fine," or "That should be no problem," or "It won't hurt," or "There is no reason for your pain." But the reality is, you need to listen to what you are feeling, and take your struggles seriously. Even your doctor may be wrong.

Keep asserting your authority until you find the help you need, especially if you are experiencing pain. If you have pain during intercourse, the cause of your pain needs to be determined and corrected. You cannot joyfully partake in sex if it hurts. One way to listen to your body is to listen to the pain and do something about it. And if you do not get the help you need from your physician, call around to find a gynecologist or urologist who is an expert in dealing with dyspareunia, that is, painful intercourse. We have seen sexual lives turned around when the woman finally stood up, represented herself, and got the help she needed.

———— ◆ ◆ ◆ ————

*Keep asserting your authority
until you find the help you need
to be able to enjoy sexual pleasure.*

———— ◆ ◆ ◆ ————

Your Husband Is Not Your Authority

Many times the man has been seen as the authority on the woman and the authority on sex. Men are innately no more expert sexually than women. Sexual expertise is learned. We hope the two of you can become authorities on yourselves and communicate your awareness of your likes and dislikes to each other. You can become sex experts with each other.

———— ◆ ◆ ◆ ————

*Become authorities on yourselves,
and communicate your awareness
of your likes and dislikes to each other.*

———— ◆ ◆ ◆ ————

Your husband can't know your sexual hungers unless you tell him. Since you are likely to change from one time to another, telling him once is not enough. He can't know whether you enjoy clitoral stimulation from his hand more than from his penis or from oral stimulation. He can't be sure, at any moment, if you prefer clitoral or intravaginal stimulation.

———— ◆ ◆ ◆ ————

*Since you are likely to change from
one time to another,
telling him once is not enough.*

———— ◆ ◆ ◆ ————

For example, your husband can't know when you are ready for entry. He may believe that your lubrication is the sign that you are ready for entry. But vaginal lubrication occurs within seconds of any erotic stimulation. Most women prefer much more love play and building of intensity in their bodies before entry. Since your emotions must be on the same track as your body, the physical signs may not indicate emotional desire or readiness for physical entry.

You can't expect that your husband will memorize a sequence that is good for you and then follow it with great faithfulness. A sexual experience is a process of two people coming together anew in each moment, just as our relationship with God is new every morning. You are discovering each other in that moment rather than following the same pattern each time. You can be and must be sensitive to each other's needs and incorporate that awareness into your experience.

———— ◆ ◆ ◆ ————

*Only you can know what your body hungers for;
you are responsible to communicate
your unique needs, idiosyncrasies, and
preferences from moment to moment.*

◆ ◆ ◆

———— ◆ ◆ ◆ ————

Your Body Is Your Authority

No one can know you as well as you know yourself. No one can tell you how you should like to be touched. Only you can discover and know what you enjoy. You can discover with your husband and communicate to him. You can't expect him to know how long or how hard or where or in what order you like to be touched. There is not a right way; there is only your way, and your way has to be discovered in your experience with each other and then shared by you as you listen to your body. Only you can take responsibility to communicate how your body wants to be touched and how you would like to make love. You are responsible to communicate your unique needs, idiosyncrasies, and preferences.

--- ◆ ◆ ◆ ---

No one can know you as well as you can learn to know yourself.

--- ◆ ◆ ◆ ---

If you don't know your body and you have little awareness of what you desire sexually, take time to discover what brings you greatest pleasure and enjoyment. You can begin with some discovery on your own, or that discovery can be a delightful experience for you to share with your husband.

--- ◆ ◆ ◆ ---

Become the best authority on your body and your sexuality.

--- ◆ ◆ ◆ ---

Learn to Listen to Your Body

How do you learn to listen to your body? You learn over time to attend to yourself from the inside and listen to the messages your body gives you. You learn to respect the signals, take them seriously, and respond to them by taking responsibility for yourself and sharing with your husband what best represents you in your lovemaking experience.

Listen All Day Long

When you are taking a shower, when you are driving in the car, when you are sitting and waiting for an appointment, when you are talking on the telephone, be aware of your body and your sexuality. Tighten and relax your vaginal muscles throughout the day. When something in your day gives you a flicker in your genitals, picture acting on that with your husband. Inform him of your flickers.

Listen to Your Desires for Sex

You may notice your desire as an urge for closeness and touch. Or you might experience yourself getting edgy or tense as an indication of your need for release. Or you may experience your sexual desire directly through genital sensations. Learn to know yourself and your sexual needs. You do have them.

Listen to Your Body During Sex

In the sexual experience, listen and communicate how you like to enjoy his body and how you like him to enjoy yours. How do you like to start? Do you prefer deep, passionate kissing, or is that better for you once you get aroused? Do you prefer to start with you pleasuring him, him pleasuring you, or mutually enjoying each other's body simultaneously? What about breast stimulation? Experiment with whether you prefer the whole breast stroked or the nipples or when in the process you shift from one to the other. If you don't like your nipples to be turned like dials on a radio, you're pretty normal. Positively invite the touch you like. If you like vigorous nipple stimulation, ask for it.

Your husband may naturally find the hot spots and go after them with even greater vigor as your arousal builds. If that's what you enjoy, affirm his natural pursuits. However, if you prefer that as you get aroused the touch gets lighter or that he take more time to enjoy the rest of your body before he hits the hot spots, you need to listen to your preferences and communicate them to him.

You may have to teach him genital touching and guide him, to some extent, in every experience. Women's genitals are very intricate and feelings are changeable. You may prefer stroking along the sides of the clitoris or general stroking of the pubic hairy mound until you get more aroused. You may invite more direct clitoral stimulation and/or intravaginal stimulation as your intensity builds. You may need to teach and talk and discover your likes with him.

You invite, but don't demand, when you want to move to entry, whether you want to engage in oral stimulation of you or him, how vigorously thrusting builds once entry takes place, how many orgasms you desire. You may not want entry, thrusting, or an orgasm. The options are completely open.

Communicate how you like to complete your sexual time together. If intercourse has occurred, you may prefer to stay united and hold each other and caress and talk. Or that can be almost irritating and painful, so you may prefer to separate and get cleaned up and get ready to fall asleep. You can express what you desire and respect what he desires and then negotiate the combination that best satisfies both.

LEARN TO LEAD

Learn to lead with your sexuality, not with demand or control. The thought of leading may be scary to you, especially if you believe that your husband should know how to please you sexually and should lead your sex life. The implication that you know your sexuality enough to lead him may make you feel uncomfortable. And he may have no more of a clue how to follow than you know how to lead. What a wonderful opportunity for the two of you to learn and discover together!

Know Your Body

Your body will point the way. So to lead, you must know your body. The starting point of knowing yourself may take a little work. To know your sexual self, you may need to go through a genital self-exam, do some reading, listen to some tapes, watch a video, or attend a seminar. Much of your discovery can happen with the two of you together if both of you have an attitude of openness and excitement to learn about yourselves and each other. As you let yourself learn, your confidence will grow, especially if he can enjoy your discovery with you.

In your discovery, identify what is true for you. Affirm the way you are similar to what we have described as true for women in general. Delineate how you are different from our findings about women. For example, most women are more verbally and aesthetically oriented. They are into communication, connection, intimacy, and spirituality more than is true for most men. You may identify with these assumptions about women or you may differ. Your uniqueness must be clarified.

Women tend to have hormonal mood and sexual interest fluctuations within the month. You have to discover your hormonal pattern. You may want to keep a monthly log of your moods, sexual interest, sexual activity, or other issues. You may find that you are most sexually interested at ovulation. Or you may discover that you are most interested right before or right after your period. Or you may have a couple of waves every month. Your pattern may be different when you're on the pill from when you're not. Knowing your hormonal cycle will be useful to you and your husband.

Your cycle is a delightful and interesting part of being a woman unless you struggle with severe PMS. If PMS interrupts your life or affects your relationships, you need medical and nutritional intervention.

Know Your Conditions

Whether or not you have ever taken time to define your conditions for sex, you do have conditions. Every person does. Women tend to have more conditions than men do. Knowing and communicating the conditions that make sex best for you will make sex better for both of you.

◆ ◆ ◆

Knowing and communicating
the conditions that make sex best for you
will make sex better for both of you.

◆ ◆ ◆

Whether your conditions are little requirements or bigger needs, they need to be respected. You may have discovered that for you the best way to get into the experience is to have a time of talking or general holding and hugging and kissing. This would not be uncommon. If connecting time leads you most naturally into the sexual experience, listen to that need, and take responsibility to make sure it happens. If being grabbed shuts you down sexually, don't let it happen. Provide him with or guide him to an alternative. Perhaps you need him to shave before sex or get up and lock the bedroom door. Or you may need very serious attention to needs that come from past sexual abuse or having been raised in an alcoholic home. If you lovingly communicate your conditions while taking responsibility for them, you will invite his respect of the conditions and bring the two of you closer together.

◆ ◆ ◆

As you lovingly communicate and take
responsibility for your conditions,
you invite his respect and
bring the two of you closer.

◆ ◆ ◆

Know Your Sexual Triggers

Sexual triggers are actions of his or yours or external situations that trigger sexual energy for you. Certain music, body pampering, and a hot, dry vacation climate are sure triggers for some women.

Many women need certain expressions from their husbands to feel valued enough to give themselves sexually. From your husband, you may need words of praise, conversation, a call of care from the office, his response to your nonsexual needs, help around the house, a love note, flowers, touch that has no sexual expectation, tender kisses, affirmation of your sexuality, or his undressing you. You probably know what "winds your clock." He would be helped if you shared your awareness with him and took responsibility for your sexual triggers.

What triggers your sexual energy today might not be the same tomorrow. Learn to discover your sexual trigger at any given moment, and have the security and confidence to express what sets you in the mood. By knowing and expressing your sexual triggers, you can learn to lead so that both of you love it.

◆ ◆ ◆

By knowing and expressing
your sexual triggers,
you learn to lead
so that both of you love it.

◆ ◆ ◆

Know Your Husband

What does sex mean to him? You may believe that all he ever thinks about is sex. As one woman put it, "Since the primary sex organ is supposed to be the brain, my husband should never have any problems with sex because that is all that is on his mind."

Some men experience love through sex. They pursue sex far more frequently than is necessary to meet their physical needs. Many times they are working on averages. They figure if they get sex once for every eight times they ask, they'll just keep asking to get the one out of eight. If this describes your husband, he may be insecure about getting love if he lets you initiate. You may need to make a deal that if a week goes by and nothing has happened, he is free to initiate.

Your husband may be quite the opposite. He may be intimidated by sex or by intimacy, and he may experience your sexual needs as pressure. You will have to be sensitive to not lead in ways that trigger his feelings of demand. For example, physical closeness and stroking of his genitals may be easier to take than a direct verbal message of your need, or just the opposite may be true for him.

If spontaneity is difficult for him, scheduling or prewarnings may work better than expecting him to respond at a moment's notice. However, if scheduling makes him feel controlled, you can plan ahead but not forewarn him. Use your preplanning to approach him in ways that you enjoy and you know will get the response you desire.

He may be anxious about his sexual adequacy. The demand men place on themselves to be competent sexually is reinforced by our society, by other men, and often by women. You can be a big help in how you lead; affirm his positive efforts. When he moves in your direction, be sure to reinforce him. Let him know how much you appreciate his remembering your needs. Even as you reinforce him, appreciate that his getting to know you will be more difficult because you are much more complex and comprehensive than he is. Also, much of what is going on for you sexually is internal, and you operate on several tracks. Your complexity may be one of the sources of his anxiety.

The very best way to lead your husband sexually is to know his emotional and sexual needs and respect them in the way you lead. According to Dr. John Gray, men need trust, acceptance, appreciation, admiration, approval, and encouragement (*Men Are from Mars, Women Are from Venus*, p. 133). As you express trust in his ability to follow your lead, acceptance of his sexuality, appreciation of his willingness to read this book and pursue his sexuality with you by serving you and letting you lead, admiration of the unique qualities he brings to your sexual relationship, approval of who he is to you, and encouragement that you believe he can be what you need him to be for you, he will indeed respond to your sexual invitations and expression of needs with strong desire to be there for you on your terms.

Learn to Take

You may have difficulty receiving sexual pleasure. You may believe that the wife's role is to please her husband. Therefore, sexual pleasure is not an expectation for you. You have accepted the myth that the woman's sexual duty is to keep the man satisfied sexually so he will not roam away from home. You may have adopted the attitude that if he is happy, you're happy. Or you may believe that nice women are not overtly sexual. You may have learned to shut down on the expression of your sexuality because of some past trauma, living with a sexually demanding husband, or the feeling you had no value to your husband other than to be the receptacle of his sexual aggression.

To learn to lead sexually in your marriage, you need to learn to take. You have to give yourself permission to take in compliments, to take in pleasure, and to take in stimulation. Sex is for you. That is the way your body is designed. God created you with a clitoris that has no other purpose in the body than to receive and transmit sexual stimulation. Even the vagina is designed for both pleasure and procreation. As you get aroused, the lower part of the vagina swells to form the orgasmic platform for pleasure, and the upper part of the vagina balloons out to hold seminal fluid and sperm to enhance impregnation. Your vagina is not just for giving pleasure to your husband's penis; it is for mutual pleasure.

A prerequisite for learning to lead is the ability to enjoy three things: (1) your own sexuality, (2) your husband's delight in your sexuality, and (3) your pleasure in his sexuality. You will actually please him more by being positively selfish in going after pleasure for yourself and taking in his enjoyment of you than by putting aside your needs and desires to try to please him.

◆ ◆ ◆

A prerequisite for learning to lead is the ability to enjoy your sexuality, your husband's delight in your sexuality, and your pleasure in his sexuality.

◆ ◆ ◆

YOUR SEXUAL RIGHTS

The Right to Be Sexual

You have the right to be sexual. Your sexuality is a wonderful gift of creation that is be enjoyed with vitality and passion. It is yours to delight in, develop, and share in the deep, warm commitment of your marriage.

The concept of sharing your body in marriage for the purpose of reveling in sexual enjoyment may seem like a secular teaching, but it is God's teaching. The passion of the Old Testament greats who are referred to as men and women of faith in Hebrews 11 and the teaching of the New Testament by the apostle Paul affirm your right to be sexual. First Corinthians 7:1–5 teaches that both men and women have sexual needs that must be taken seriously by husbands and wives. The mystery of sexuality is presented in Ephesians 5. Because it is a right of marriage, you are not to withhold from each other, and you are to delight in each other as Christ does the church and hopes the church does in Him.

The Right to Pleasure and Satisfaction

The right to be sexual includes the right to receive sexual pleasure and satisfaction. Even though sex is certainly for procreation, it is for pleasure and satisfaction. If, according to 1 Corinthians 7, you are not to withhold sex from each other except by agreement for special times of prayer and then come together quickly to avoid sexual temptation, you are expected to have sex for your sexual needs, not for having babies and not just for your husband's needs. Otherwise, the instruction would have been to be sure you are together often enough to be able to conceive and would have been only for you not to withhold from your husband. The command is mutual.

The majority of the time, sex is for pleasure. The expectation of sexual pleasure in marriage is assumed throughout the Scriptures and is certainly your right. Sex is not just for the man's pleasure; it is for the pleasure of both partners. Since the woman's sexual enjoyment gives the man the greatest pleasure, you certainly have the right to go after pleasure for yourself. By pleasure, we mean the capacity to take in and enjoy all the sensations that are yours to enjoy as a result of how your body and spirit were designed.

You have the right and the responsibility to know and go after what brings you the greatest pleasure and fulfillment. You may need to learn to freely express your needs and use your body to pursue fulfillment. As you become comfortable with going after pleasure, you will open up new vistas of connection and delight for the two of you.

You have the sexual right to *take as much time as you need*. Asking for time for your pleasure and fulfillment may cause turmoil inside you. You may say, "I don't deserve it; that will take too much time. I need three hours before my engines get revved." But it is absolutely essential that you take the time you need if sex is going to be a fulfilling experience for both of you throughout your marriage.

SEX RESPONSE PATTERN

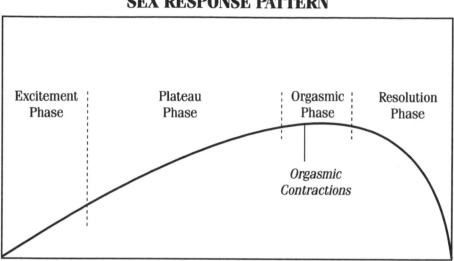

You have the right to *be free to respond in your way*. If you respond in waves, peaks and dips, a gradual incline, or shoot straight up like a firecracker, allow your body to follow its natural rhythm. There is no right or wrong way. You may express your orgasms very quietly and internally or with a lot of yelling and screaming. Within the boundaries of having taken the proper precautions for privacy from your children, neighbors, and others, you are free to pursue your response and expressions of that response within the context of what works in your marriage. Compare your response patterns with the graphs on page 192. You might draw graph lines to represent your various patterns of response.

The Right to Heal from Violation

Finally, you have the right to *take time to heal from violation*. You cannot be expected to fulfill your responsibilities for sex in marriage until you have healed sexually. If you were sexually or physically abused as a child, a victim of trauma, from an alcoholic home, in an abusive relationship as an adolescent or adult, or raped, it is imperative that you accept the reality that you will need time to heal. Your right to take time to heal is completely understandable and acceptable and one of your sexual rights.

GRAPHS OF VARIOUS RESPONSE PATTERNS

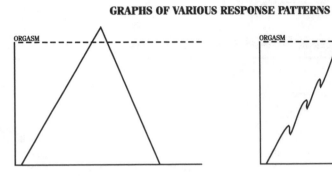

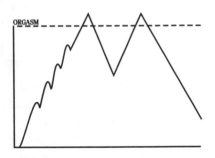

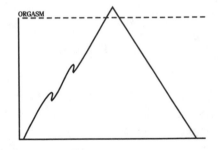

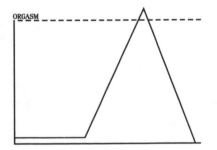

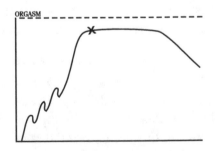

◆ ◆ ◆

*You cannot be expected to fulfill
your biblical responsibilities for
sex in marriage until you have
healed from your past.*

◆ ◆ ◆

Your Rights as a Couple

Other rights may be unique to you, to your husband, or to both of you as a couple. Talk together about each of your individual and your couple rights and responsibilities in sex. Each of you probably has ideas of your sexual rights and responsibilities for sex in marriage, but you may have no notion what the other believes. Clarifying your similarities and differences can open a whole way of expressing and enjoying yourselves sexually.

YOU CAN'T WATCH AND PLAY AT THE SAME TIME

The more you attend to how you are doing, the more you will get in the way of your body's experience. Sex works best when you get lost in the enjoyment of each other and satisfy the hunger inside you rather than watch your body or his response.

◆ ◆ ◆

*Sex works best when you get
lost in the enjoyment of each other
and satisfy the hunger inside you.*

◆ ◆ ◆

Spectatoring will keep you from being a participant. One woman asked us to help her determine what was getting in the way of her sexual arousal and release with her husband. We asked her to picture exactly what they did and what she felt in response to their activities. She led us through their last sexual event. She reported following every action with an evaluation of her body's response rather than a feeling from inside. For example, she said, "When he stroked me all over my body, I got lubricated. But his touching my clitoris did nothing. Then when I asked him to go inside my vagina, I got aroused, so I told him and everything stopped." She had stopped her body's automatic responses by mentally going outside herself and watching her body's response to their activities. She was spectatoring.

Another woman watched her husband. She reported his level of enthusiasm or boredom. She watched whether he had his eyes open or closed, whether he seemed excited enough, or whether he was pleased with her level of responsiveness. She distracted from her body's response by going outside herself and indirectly evaluating herself through him.

You cannot watch and expect your body to respond. Watching interrupts pleasure and response because it creates self-consciousness and performance anxiety. Self-consciousness inhibits the natural body responses, and performance anxiety gets in the way of performance.

Evaluation negatively affects every aspect of the sexual experience. Whether counting how many times you are together per week, how long it takes, who initiated last time, or how many orgasms you had—all attending will get in the way of abandonment and delight in sex.

To counteract watching, become an active player because you can't watch and play at the same time. As you get into the active role and vigorously pursue the pleasure that is yours to enjoy and his to delight in, you will find greater pleasure and fulfillment, and so will he.

◆ ◆ ◆

To counteract watching, become an active player because you can't watch and play at the same time.

◆ ◆ ◆

LEAD HIM TO INTIMACY

Long-term intimacy is developed throughout a relationship when the woman can connect with where the man is and lead him to greater intimacy.

The woman usually comes to marriage with a greater capacity for intimacy than does the man.

Your Capacity for Intimacy

Growing up, girls develop the capacity for intimacy in ways that often aren't as available or as natural for boys. Girls tend to share more time with their mothers than boys do with their fathers. Girls work out their emotions by talking with each other; boys tend to process their feelings in seclusion. Girls form relationships with their dolls, teddy bears, and imaginary friends. Boys may attach to a stuffed animal or other "friend" for comfort or security, but they are not as likely to relate to the inanimate object as though it were an intimate friend. Girls and women have greater needs and capacity for spiritual and nurturing relationship skills, which are the basis for intimacy.

Your Need to Nurture Intimacy

If you identify with the typical differences between men and women, you serve your relationship best by assuming that you need to nurture intimacy. Your felt need for and comfort with ongoing intimate connection may be greater than his. You may need to lead him to the closeness he enjoys when it happens. Even if he won you by writing poetry or singing songs to you up on the balcony when he was courting, his loss of that skill is not really a loss. There is a big difference for him between courting that conquers and intimacy that builds.

Accept His Need for Space

In pursuing intimacy with your husband, you need to accept that he will get close and then slip back to needing space and then be ready to move into a little closer contact again. If you think in electrical terms, a man works best with an alternating current of closeness and intimacy rather than a direct current. He tends to short out with a direct current of ongoing intimacy, much like a woman shorts out with an ongoing direct current of clitoral stimulation. The times of alternating need vary from person to person and from day to day.

What do we mean by alternating? Talking in fifteen-minute or half-hour blocks of time with a good bit of space in between will be much more manageable for a lot of men than an hour-and-a-half or two-hour discussion. Sharing for an extended period of time every few days is going to be a lot easier than daily in-depth conversations.

And this is Stan's private library.

Balance Your Needs and His Needs

A man is likely to be distracted from his need for or openness to intimacy by male activities. A game that's important to him, a fishing trip, or a day for golf can become a priority over intimacy with you. You may feel replaced. Don't think of his need as a message about you. He would be exactly the same whoever he was married to. As you are able to accept his male needs and still ask for your needs, the two of you can find ways to get both met. He will be able to give more to you as you accept his needs for maleness. Planning your timing so that it takes into account both spouses' needs is vital.

A man usually prefers that you don't announce your intimacy times by a statement such as, "Let's share," "Let's communicate," or "Let's be intimate." Rather than spotlighting your intimacy attempts and creating self-consciousness, start doing it in the context of your daily life together or at scheduled talk times.

Sex: An Avenue of Intimacy for Men

Having sex can be an easier form of intimacy for a man. Having physical closeness will often open the door to emotional closeness for him. Connecting communication and sharing times with sexual times will be important on occasion. However, you need to have times that are solely focused on connecting through communication rather than always using sex for that purpose.

Romance: An Avenue of Intimacy for Women

A woman may have romantic images of how the marriage relationship and sexual life should be. You may not have shared these images with your husband, but you are frustrated that he doesn't fulfill the romantic dreams. Take responsibility to communicate and see to it that your need to be romantic or set up an atmosphere happens.

You may say, "But how can romance be romantic if I do it?" If you create your vision of romance, it will be romantic. If you expect him to intuitively know what you consider romantic, you will be disappointed, and he will lose confidence in trying.

Or you may think, *If he loved me, he would do the romantic part.* His romantic attentiveness or lack of romantic ability probably has nothing to do with love. The way a man's brain works and his comfort with romantic efforts are more vital to what he does or doesn't do than how much he loves you or cares for you.

Romance will be most satisfying when you take the responsibility to make it happen. If you absolutely need him to create the romance for you, set aside a time to talk about your need with him, and together make a plan for what you need that he can fulfill. It may be helpful to let him know the small expressions of romance you would like. You may feel special when he opens the doors for you. Let him know, with a fun and loving spirit, that from now on when you're out on a date, you're going to stand by a door until he opens it.

As he attempts to take action on the plan, reinforce his efforts. Keep in mind that particularly in the sexual realm, a man's self-worth is intricately interwoven. A man feels like a man when he perceives that he has been a good lover. He will perceive himself as a good lover when he has been able to give you what you asked and you were appreciative of his efforts. With time, he may even create some romance on his own.

Romance isn't only about flying to the Mediterranean on a private jet. It's also about the tiny things of touch and thoughtfulness and courtesies you demonstrate to each other.

Blocks to Intimacy

When your husband's self-worth is totally tied up in your sexual response, performance demands will interrupt sexual pleasure, intimacy and, eventually, desire. Intimacy will be replaced with attempts to please and anxiety about not being what he needs you to be. He will need to take responsibility to break his part of the dilemma as described in chapter 6. Your responsibility will be to ask for the space you need while reassuring him that you desire sexual pleasure and intimacy without demands to meet his needs. Keep with your sexuality, and pursue your sexual desires with him when possible.

The anger, shame, abuse, abandonment, or low self-esteem issues that we talked about as interfering with intimacy could be your issues as well as his. One woman stated that she had no intention or wish to pursue her sexuality for herself because she knew that would make her husband happy. She would rather not have pleasure if her pleasure had the possibility of being positive for him. You may have brought destructive patterns into the marriage. If that is the case, you may do well to seek professional help to sort through those issues.

Sex may have become the battleground for working out other marital or personal issues. These issues interrupt your intimacy. When couples come for sexual therapy, we are often surprised to discover that the spouses' desires for their sexual life are almost identical, even though their perception is that they are miles apart. Other issues have invaded the sexual realm and have distorted their perceptions of their mutual desire for sexual intimacy and pleasure.

You will need to work as a couple to sort out the issues interfering with the intimacy you both desire. You may need professional help. Once you can identify the real issues, make plans to correct your destructive relationship patterns that are showing up in the bedroom. As you overcome the invading obstacles, intimacy will develop.

WHEN IT ISN'T WORKING

Each of you brings a unique history and personality to your sexual life. Sometimes that uniqueness may interfere with the love, passion, and intimacy God intended for you in your marriage. What if your sex life is not working as it's supposed to?

What If He Wants It and You Don't?

Both of you were created as sexual beings, male and female. You were designed to desire sexual closeness, arousal, and release. How often should you feel desire? There is no exact number for you. However, if you do not periodically sense some urge or urgency in your body for sexual contact, pleasure, arousal, or release, you need to attend to that absence.

When the urge to be close, to be aroused, or to have release is lacking or severely diminished, it is our assumption that life's events, bodily functioning, or relationship issues have gotten in the way of the natural flow or your awareness of sexual desire. It may be a result of how you were raised, some violating experience that occurred for you as you were growing up or even once you had grown up, inadequate hormonal balance, or a troubled relationship. Whatever it is, you can deal with it, but only you can take responsibility for it and get the help you need.

Helen tries out her new "Not-Tonight-Honey" nightgown.

What If "Going for It" Is Giving In to Him?

You know how much he would like it if you enjoyed sex, got aroused, had orgasms, or were an active respondent, so you can't do it. You can't enjoy your sexuality for yourself because it really is for him; your response is too important to him. Or like the woman we mentioned earlier, maybe you won't let yourself do it if it gives him any pleasure. Your anger toward him keeps you from going for sex for yourself.

One woman stated, "I wouldn't initiate sex whenever I wanted it. I would be afraid that if I had it whenever I wanted it, he would get used to having it too often." She withholds from her own pleasure because of fear that he would then become expectant, and his expectation would cause her demand to perform for him. You may not go for sex for yourself because you are afraid of your desire turning to demand to please him.

Maybe the bondage of your anger toward your husband keeps you from discovering love, passion, and intimacy. That bondage is probably much older than your relationship with your husband. It probably started with forced early sexuality in your home. You may have had inappropriate exposure to your father, to other men your mother brought into your home, to a male baby-sitter, or some other early sexual exposure.

One woman who was trapped by her bondage had a father who sexualized her from as long as she could remember. She experienced emotional incest and inappropriate sexuality with her father throughout her adolescent and young adult years. In a sense, she learned to use her body to get his attention.

Another woman had her father's sexuality forced on her with the disguise, and probably the belief of her parents, that it was for her good. She was forced to watch her father urinate when she was a toddler and preschooler to teach her about male genitals. She and her father went on camping trips, which she loved to do with him, but as an adult, she discovered that he would masturbate in the bed next to her bed. During her dating, she had sex forced on her before she was ready and eager for sex. That man became her husband. As her husband, he pushed for sex, watched her response, and got his affirmation from her sexual interest and responsiveness. For her to see sex as something for herself seemed almost impossible.

Still another woman's mother showed her adult genitals to her as a young child to teach her what her genitals would look like when she grew up. One woman's mother used ritualistic cleaning of her genitals. Another woman's mother pinched her budding breasts regularly to check their development and determine need for bra size. All of these women had their sexuality taken away from them as children or adolescents. Now they have difficulty going for sex for themselves.

Women who have had their sexuality taken away from them demonstrate their angry, sexual withholding by sabotaging their sexual progress. One woman stated the feeling: "I don't even want to want sex with him." These women come to therapy to get "healed," but they fail (always for seemingly legitimate reasons) to follow the suggested treatment plan that could change their dilemma, yet they feel trapped by their sexual dysfunction. They want sexual freedom, but they can't pursue it because it would also benefit their husbands.

◆ ◆ ◆

Release yourself from the bondage of withholding from your pleasure because your pleasure would bring him pleasure.

◆ ◆ ◆

Your angry bondage that restricts your sexuality may be anger because you lost your father between ages four and thirteen. Whether he died or just left, you feel that he deserted you. Or maybe your father was never there for you; he was always critical. There is no way you can allow yourself to freely pursue sex with a man as close to you as your husband. Subconsciously, you fear he would leave you, as your father did. So you keep a safe distance in your relationship by always being angry with him; you cannot let yourself be sexual with him. You may be attracted to and tempted by other men, but you can't be sexual with your husband. You believe it is because of how he is. And likely he has his faults and limitations, but they are probably not the real reasons for your inability to go after sex for yourself in your marriage.

Your bondage tends to trigger his insecurity. Sex then becomes more than sex for him (see chapter 6). He starts investing more and more in your sexual interest and responsiveness. The more important your response becomes to him, the angrier you get and the more you withhold. The more you withhold, the more he pursues sex, evaluates your interest, and watches your response.

Even though you bring the primary issues that cause this struggle between you, it will seem that he is the cause of your difficulty of not being free to pursue sex for yourself. So he will have to back off before you can experience your own sexuality for your pleasure. When you learn to enjoy sex for yourself, he will relax and not be an anxious pursuer or evaluator. As long as you withhold yourself, he will tend to anxiously check or pursue. It is a tough cycle to break!

◆ ◆ ◆

When you are able to free yourself to pursue sex for yourself, your husband will relax and stop anxiously pursuing and evaluating your sexuality.

◆ ◆ ◆

What If My Mind Wanders?

Your mind will wander during sex. Your husband's may, also, but not as frequently. When a man is aroused, his mind is usually connected with his body. Since you function on two tracks, you can enjoy bodily pleasure at the same time that a mundane thought can enter your mind. You may think about the grocery list, the wallpaper you need, or what you're going to pack in the kids' lunches tomorrow, or you may remember something you need to tell your husband. Even though sharing your mundane thoughts with your husband will tend to detract, do not beat yourself up about your passing thoughts as long as they do not distract from your pleasure or take you away from the experience.

When a wandering mind distracts from your pleasure or experience, you can counteract it by getting active. Besides the fact that you function on two tracks, your mind wanders more than your husband's because you tend to be more passive than he is. If you talk, if you move, if you assume the leading role of listening to your body hungers and go after them, it is not likely that your mind will wander beyond passing thoughts or pictures. If your wandering interrupts pleasure in any way, change positions, get on top, talk, move, or tease. Try whatever you can to shift from the passive mode where your mind isn't being kept engaged with your body to a mode where you are vigorously and vitally involved.

What If He Has the Headache?

A man may lack sexual interest. When diminished sexual desire becomes the pattern rather than the exception, you need to pursue a solution so that the underlying causes can be understood and corrected.

Lack of sexual desire in a man may be due to reasons similar to those true for a woman. He may have suffered past abuse or failure, be troubled by the marital relationship, struggle with internal turmoil about being sexual, or not perceive himself as a successful lover. Preoccupation with some other form of sexual expression, such as homosexuality, pornography, or other sexual addictions, could also cause a man not to be interested in making love with his wife.

You may take action by supporting and participating with your husband in determining and correcting his lack of desire. The two of you may do that on your own or you may seek professional help.

What If He Keeps Forgetting What I've Told Him?

Men may forget during sex for the same reason that their minds are not likely to wander; their minds and bodies are totally connected to their arousal and release. They are not on two tracks.

Whatever the cause of his forgetting, it is not likely a sign of his lack of love and care for you. Thus, both of you will benefit if you can assume responsibility to let him know and go after what you desire during your sexual times together. If he forgets that it hurts you when he squeezes your nipples, when he hooks his finger into the vagina, or when he latches onto one spot and rubs it until it feels like it's going to ignite, gently guide his hand or body contact to an area or activity that is pleasurable for you. Try to take action before you reach the point of distancing irritability.

Your assuming responsibility for yourself is not to let him off the hook. He also needs to be responsible for how he behaves and what he does. His chapters will help him with his part. But he cannot do his part without your active involvement.

What If We Have Sex the Same Way Every Time?

Repetition is safe, predictable, and known. The predictability of having sex exactly the same way every time may bring a kind of security because each knows the role and what works or doesn't work. Yet one or both of you may be discontented with your repetitive pattern.

Change is difficult even if you want the newness and spark that come with change. Change takes work. You may already feel overwhelmed with your life responsibilities. Your sex life may be comfortable the way it is, so you hesitate to try something new that has the risk of failure. Maybe you'd like to change, but you're concerned about his response to your change. Also, change takes risk. You may be afraid of the results of the change.

To change from having sex the same way every time, you need to talk to each other and make a plan. One of you may need to assume leadership in bringing creativity into your sex life. Look at the rest of your lives to determine who is most likely to experiment with newness. You may be married to a man who does exactly the same thing every day when he gets home from work, likes to eat the same meals at the same time, goes to the same restaurants, and does the same chores and activities on Saturday. So why would he be any different in the lovemaking department? If change is important for you, you will probably have to see to it that change happens. He likely will not succeed in bringing about the creative differences. On the other hand, if you're the stuck-in-the-mud person, he may have to be more innovative. If neither of you can muster up enough originality to make the changes your sexual relationship needs, use our book *52 Ways to Have Fun, Fantastic Sex*.

What If All We Ever Have Is Quickies?

Quickies are a necessity in today's world of overcommitment. But they might be thought of as a junk food snack to tide you over until the real

thing comes along. So, your sexual relationship will not survive on quickies alone.

What can you do if your sexual experiences are between six and seven
minutes long and happen late at night or perhaps even in the middle of the
night? You can take several approaches. The first step is to talk about your
pattern and what each of you would like to do about it. If having longer,
quality sexual times is a mutual goal, we encourage you to set aside times
when you focus just on pleasuring and caressing each other. If he isn't willing to take that time, you may look for opportunities to focus on pleasuring him. Make your attempts a playful game so that the two of you can
move to the place where you can enjoy teasing about it.

What If My Sexual Past Has Invaded Our Bedroom?

A sexual past has a way of invading the bedroom. When there has been
serious sexual pain in the past, it usually gets in the way in the present. It
gets in the way by coming up in your mind when you are reminded of the
abusive or painful event. The effects of that past may be conscious or half
conscious or sometimes totally unconscious, but you find yourself closing
up.

If your past is your struggle, you must get outside help. You may see an
individual therapist or join a group of women who have had similar experiences.

Sharing the pain is going to help get past the pain. Some women are
fearful that if they share their pain from the past, they will drive their
husbands away. We don't find that to be true. Instead, we find that most
husbands are extremely open and ready to be involved to help their
wives deal with the pain so that they can totally enjoy the sexual experience.

If certain sexual activities are reminders of the abuse, avoid them. For
example, if making love in the dark reminds you of the abuse of your past,
make love in the daytime or with the lights on. If a certain touch or a certain noise cues off a panicky avoidant reaction in you, plan ways to signal
him so that he can make the appropriate adjustments. Sometimes major
shifts are necessary. If you were abused when you were on your back, you
may be able to let go to orgasm only if you are on top.

You cannot just forget your painful past. You need to deal with it. If you
and he can deal with your past together and out loud, your path to healing
will be a journey you take with your husband at your side.

What If We Don't Talk About Sex?

Talking about sex is vital to keeping love, passion, and intimacy alive in your sex life. Yet many couples have not learned to share openly with each other about sex. They did not learn to talk about sex in their homes, they cannot find the correct words to express themselves, and they are afraid of embarking on such an emotionally loaded dimension of their relationship.

———— ◆ ◆ ◆ ————

Talking about sex is vital to keeping
love, passion, and intimacy alive in your sex life.

———— ◆ ◆ ◆ ————

To open the topic of your sexual relationship, choose the setting in which talking is most comfortable. If most of your more intimate relationship conversations have happened away from home, use a time away. Maybe you would both rather walk and talk or drive and talk than sit and look at each other and talk. If you have had your best talk times early in the morning or late at night, choose the time that is most likely to work.

Decide on a medium of communication that will be most effective. Maybe you both can write better and then read each other's writings and talk about them. Maybe you would each like to talk into a tape recorder and listen and react to each other. You may find it easiest to interact by reading aloud to each other.

Women tend not to talk about sex after sex. They seem to have difficulty or don't think about expressing their enjoyment after a nice sexual time. They are more focused on the process itself, and they do not think about the result of the process as men do. Since doing good at sex is important for men and doing good is equated with having a happy wife, an expression of your enjoyment or pleasure after a time together would be a little effort you could take to enhance your sexual life.

Talking after sex about sex may be for you like talking about our sexual therapy is for Joyce. We both love our work, but Cliff really enjoys keeping track of how many hours each of us saw clients and how much income each brought in, and comparing how we did last month to this month or a year ago this month. Cliff's enjoyment places pressure on Joyce to perform. His attention to how we are doing feels like evaluation. If you feel evaluated by talking about your experience afterward, think about ways to express your pleasure without evaluation. It works for Joyce to be excited about how her practice is going, but it stifles her for Cliff to keep records on her performance.

Talking about your sex life is an absolute must for a healthy sexual relationship. The willingness to share your intimate feelings about this vulnerable area of your marriage and the ability to listen to each other communicate a message of care that is very significant. It affirms a bond in your relationship and expresses a form of intimacy. As you relax with each other and the topic, you will find yourselves sharing your dreams and discovering new creativity and stimulation relationally and sexually.

———————   ◆ ◆ ◆   ———————

Talking about your sexual relationship
without evaluation expresses care, creates a bond,
develops intimacy, and sparks dreams, creativity,
and stimulation both relationally and sexually.

———————   ◆ ◆ ◆   ———————

What If I Can't Be Sexual?

You may be concerned that none of these words to wives will work for you. You have been trying all of your married life and you're convinced you just are not sexual. Maybe God left out the sexual lobe when He created your brain. Your body may respond, but you don't feel anything; you are not emotionally connected to the arousal that does occur in your body. Or maybe you try and try, and nothing happens to your body.

For some women, to be overtly sexual is frightening. "I can't tell him when I'm turned on. I wouldn't want to initiate sex because that would be a sign of my neediness." These words were expressed by a woman who can be sexually responsive by herself through masturbation, but cannot with her husband. She would like to respond with him. Her mother had many sexual partners after Dad left them when she was two years old. Her dad left her and her mother needy and being sexually out of control was her mother's way of showing her neediness to the daughter. She is now an adult woman struggling in her sexual relationship with her husband.

Other women have blocked their ability to receive, sometimes both in life and in sex. "I can enjoy pleasing him, but I don't think I can receive," stated one woman after she had tried for the third time to guide her husband and talk to him about what sexual touching she would enjoy. The first time she tried, she got so upset that she thought of the experience as a disaster. We reassured her that we had learned much from her reaction to her attempt, so we affirmed her success in trying. The second time she tried to teach him, she stated that it didn't work because none of the places he touched her got her aroused. Once again, we were pleased that she was able to complete the total experience of guiding his hands over the front of her body, and we explained that arousal was not likely in a clinical teaching experience. The third time, she felt some feelings, but she rushed through to focus on him. We continued to recommend that she learn to focus on the sensation of where his hand was touching her skin and take in his touch—that is all.

There may also be a hormonal reason for your inability to be sexual. Since attending a conference for sexual therapists from around the country, we have been encouraging physicians to evaluate our female clients' hormonal levels. At the conference, Dr. Lonnie Barbach reported finding that women who have pain during intercourse, low sexual desire, and/or difficulty responding sexually often are found to have low normal or below normal free or available testosterone levels. The women who have been tested from our practice have confirmed that finding. There is a solution. Applying a testosterone cream that your physician can prescribe and order from the Women's International Pharmacy out of Madison, Wisconsin, will gradually make a difference. The cream is applied once or twice daily to the vulva. If your physician is not aware of this information, have him contact us (818-449-2525). If he or she is not open to assessing your need for or to prescribing hormonal treatment, the Women's International Pharmacy may be able to refer you to another physician in your area (800-279-5708).

You may not be able to allow yourself to be sexual because of fear of your sexuality, inability to receive sexual pleasure, or demands you and/or your husband have placed on you to be sexual. Once you recognize the reason that you have not been able to be sexual and have eliminated or taken care of any hormonal deficits, you still will need to decide to be sexual.

Accept that by God's design and creation you are sexual. Start behaving sexually. The actions will precede the feelings. Give yourself at least a year of consistently pursuing sex for yourself before you get discouraged. Learn to verbalize and distract from your negative thoughts that this will never happen to me. Tell your husband when such thoughts interrupt your pleasure. Know that you will yearn to have the urge, the desire, and the feelings, but continually recommit yourself to pursue by decision, not by desire. Allow him the enjoyment of your body, whether your body responds or not, and enjoy his body, even if you don't get aroused by it.

What If He Doesn't Turn Me On?

He cannot turn you on. Only you can allow your body to get turned on. With the exception of the hormonal issue, whether or not you allow response is your decision. To allow yourself to be turned on by him, you need to be ready to totally give yourself to him.

You may want to get turned on, but you don't want to give yourself to him. You cannot have both; it's your choice. You may need to deal with conflict or anger in your relationship or issues from your past. You may need to take an inventory of what has changed since the time in your relationship when you did allow yourself to respond to him. Maybe sex has always been disappointing. Or maybe he has never taken enough time. Or you've never been able to respond, no matter how much time he has taken. Or maybe you are bored with your sex life.

If you don't respond to him the way you used to, usually something has changed in the relationship so that you no longer have the natural connected feelings that allow you to give yourself sexually. Perhaps something has happened inside you to cause you to shut down. You will have to take deliberate steps to know yourself and pursue the issues that shut you down if you are going to bring about some of the old response that you enjoyed.

What If I'm Not in Love with Him?

Love is a decision, a commitment. Your feelings of love can change from day to day. Love can be hurt. You may decide to no longer love because of hurts, but that is your decision, not something that happens to you. To love him or not to love him is in your control.

We have discovered in marital therapy that when the barriers between a couple can be broken down, their decision of love can be rekindled, and the feeling of "in loveness" can return. Nevertheless, the feelings come and go. The feelings cannot be the criteria for true love. Certainly, the feelings enhance the decision to love, and they should be taken seriously. But do not think that the relationship is over because you feel that you are no longer in love with him.

Try loving him according to 1 Corinthians 13: Don't give up, care more for him than you care for yourself, don't want what you don't have, don't strut, don't have a swelled head, don't force yourself on him, don't insist on "me first," don't fly off the handle, don't keep score of his wrongdoings, don't revel when he grovels, take pleasure in the truth, put up with anything, trust God always, and always look for the best (adapted from *The Message* by Eugene H. Peterson).

PROTECT YOUR MARRIAGE

Practicing the commitment of love, pursuing your sexuality with your husband, and applying the same recommendations we wrote to your husband on affair proofing your marriage are keys to protecting your marriage. All women are vulnerable to affairs, just as all men are. So you, too, need to attend to your vulnerability. When you are tempted outside your marriage, turn the spark toward home, and act on it with your husband. Plan that erotic adventure with him, just as we encouraged him to plan one with you. You, too, can design and shape your married sexual life to have excitement, passion, intrigue, and intimacy that an affair promises to deliver but never does.

HAVE AS MUCH FUN AS HE DOES

Fun is fun only when the two of you are enjoying yourselves together. You can't have much fun alone, so share in your capacity to be innovative and experimental. If your mind wanders to doing the dishes, imagine that you're doing the dishes in the nude when he comes home. Use your mind, use your body, and use your spirit to enjoy and delight in each other.

Lighten Up

Learn to laugh and cry together. Some situations can seem so impossible, you may have that feeling of crying and laughing at the same time. As long as you're together in your laughter, you will lead in lightening the situation. It won't work for you to laugh if he is deadly serious.

Turn a struggle into a game. For example, if you have been practicing listening to your body and pursuing its natural responses in order to allow an orgasm, have him pant and breathe heavily with you. Make facial grimaces like you're trying to scare him. Moan and groan together. Instead of gritting your teeth and trying to have an orgasm, which never works anyway, go for fun and games. You can do similar games in working with him on learning ejaculatory control. Name "Charlie." Talk to Charlie. Let him tell you the numbers of the level of his arousal by indicating that Charlie is going for a seven so you'd better give him a squeeze. Make work fun.

Fantasize Together

Use your imagination. Your capacity to fantasize can bring a whole world of possibilities to your love life and certainly is a distraction from performance anxiety or demands to respond. Create and share your fantasies aloud with him. Imagine yourselves to be something you could never be. Picture yourselves in places you will never visit. Create activities you don't feel like doing. Have fun in the privacy of your home.

Play

Keep your childlike spirits alive in your sexual relationship. Roll, giggle, tickle, and tease with respect. Be silly. Exaggerate. Have times of playful snuggling and caressing that are totally carefree.

The fun of sex is not to trivialize sex, but to expand your range of sexual and sensual enjoyment within the context of your marital relationship. Sometimes life will be filled with circumstances that are too serious to allow playfulness. Respect those times. The attitude is one of openness to each other in the moment.

We cannot emphasize enough how vital it is for you to give yourself permission to be the vibrant sexual person God designed you to be. You may have to make the decision before you will experience your sexuality. As you take responsibility for your sexuality—to know it and to share it with your husband—you will discover true love, passion, and intimacy in your marriage.

A good woman is hard to find,
and worth far more than diamonds.
Her husband trusts her without reserve,

and never has reason to regret it.
Never spiteful, she treats him generously
all her life long
(Prov. 31:10–12, *The Message*).

Men Make the Difference

Men make the difference in sex in marriage. Women set the boundaries before marriage. Men have the key to unlock the boundaries within the love and commitment of marriage. The key to a woman's sexuality is affirmation. When a woman believes she is a vibrant sexual person, she will exude sexuality. Her husband is the person in the world most able to convince her that she is a sexual person. He convinces her most by his enjoyment of her.

The best guarantee to keep you together for a lifetime is your delight in each other—the positive moments you acquire. You can bicker and have differences, but when you affirm each other with your attention and affection, the tensions of the day melt away.

Sex is a small, but significant, ingredient in the formula of marriage. When sex is a mutually satisfying dimension of your marriage, it claims about 10 percent or 20 percent of your energy. It is the lubricant that smooths the other issues in the marriage. When one or both of you are troubled by your sex life, sex looms large, occupying somewhere between 80 percent and 90 percent of your energy.

Since sex is so easily conditioned, most adults come to marriage already well set in their sexual patterns of thinking and responding. When they are healthy patterns that affirm spirituality and sexuality in both the man and the woman, the delights of the sexual union will develop and grow with a little education and direction. When the patterns got started prematurely or were associated with inappropriate stimuli, new patterns will have to be established. The man, as the servant leader, will be responsible to make sure positive patterns of sexuality and spirituality can be developed. You will do that by gaining knowledge, opening communication with your wife, and learning to know yourself and your wife at a deep, intimate level.

We are convinced that a positive sexual life, although not necessary for a good marriage, adds incredible vibrancy and fluency to marriage. We believe all marriages are capable of a mutually satisfying sexual life. Attaining that potential will be more the responsibility of the husband than the wife. We have found that when you as the man are willing and able to change, the sexual relationship in marriage improves, even if your wife is a greater contributor to what needs to change.

The Promise Keepers movement is sweeping the nation and empowering men of God of all ages to take a stand for men in relation to God, their mentors, their integrity, their marriage and family, the church, their brothers, and their world. We are convinced that this and other expressions of the men's movement have set the stage for men of God to accept their responsibility to love their wives as Christ loved the church and be able to apply that teaching to the marriage bed. *Men and Sex* will help men apply *servant leadership* to their marital sex lives. As they do, they will accept their natural instincts and those of their wives, as they differ and as they blend, and they will become the validators of women's sexuality in marriage.

As men accept their power to validate their wives' sexuality and enhance their marital sexual relationships, the potential for couples staying together for a lifetime will increase. Marital commitments will be sealed by the passionate, intimate, and loving connection that transpires when the woman allows all of her sexuality because the man delights in her. Together they are freed to experience the joy of being truly one flesh— one heart, one soul, one mind, and one strength to the glory of God!

Bibliography

Barbach, Lonnie. *For Yourself: The Fulfillment of Female Sexuality.* New York: Doubleday, 1975.

———. *The Pause: Positive Approaches to Menopause.* New York: Penguin, 1993.

Buford, Bob. *Halftime: Changing Your Game Plan from Success to Significance.* Grand Rapids, Mich.: Zondervan, 1994.

Buscaglia, Leo. *Loving Each Other: The Challenge of Human Relationships.* New York: Holt, Rinehart & Winston, 1984.

Carnes, Patrick. *Contrary to Love: Helping the Sexual Addict.* Minneapolis: CompCare Publishers, 1989.

———. *Out of the Shadows: Understanding Sexual Addiction.* Minneapolis: CompCare Publishers, 1983.

Cousins, Norman. *Anatomy of an Illness.* New York: Norton, 1979.

———. *Head First.* New York: Penguin, 1990.

Dillow, Joseph C. *Solomon on Sex.* Nashville: Thomas Nelson, 1977.

Dobson, James C. *Love for a Lifetime: Building a Marriage That Will Go the Distance.* Portland: Multnomah, 1987.

Fromm, Erich. *The Art of Loving.* New York: Harper & Row, 1956.

Gallwey, W. Timothy. *The Inner Game of Tennis.* New York: Random House, 1974.

Gilder, George. *Men and Marriage.* Gretna: Pelican Publishing Co., 1986.

Godek, Gregory J. P. *1001 Ways to Be Romantic.* Weymouth, Mass.: Casablanca, 1991.

Gottman, John. *Why Marriages Succeed or Fail.* New York: Simon & Schuster, 1994.

Gray, John. *Mars and Venus in the Bedroom: A Guide to Lasting Romance and Passion.* New York: HarperCollins, 1995.

———. *Men Are from Mars, Women Are from Venus.* New York: HarperCollins, 1992.

Hart, Archibald D. *The Hidden Link Between Adrenaline and Stress.* Dallas: Word, 1986.

———. *The Sexual Man.* Dallas: Word, 1994.

Hayden, Naura. *How to Satisfy a Woman Every Time . . . and Have Her Beg for More!* New York: Penguin, 1982.

Heiman, Julia R., and Joseph LoPiccolo. *Becoming Orgasmic*. New York: Prentice Hall, 1988.

Hendrix, Harville. *Getting the Love You Want*. New York: Harper & Row, 1990.

Hughes, R. Kent. *Disciplines of a Godly Man*. Wheaton, Ill.: Crossway Books, 1991.

Kaplan, Helen Singer. *PE: How to Overcome Premature Ejaculation*. New York: Brunner/Mazel, 1979.

Laaser, Mark. *The Secret Sin*. Grand Rapids, Mich.: Zondervan, 1992.

Ladas, A. K., B. Whipple, and I. D. Perry. *The G Spot*. New York: Holt, Rinehart & Winston, 1982.

Love, Patricia. *Hot Monogamy*. New York: Penguin, 1995.

Masters, William H., and Virginia E. Johnson. *Human Sexual Inadequacy*. Boston: Little, Brown, 1970.

May, Rollo. *Love and Will*. New York: Norton, 1969.

McCarthy, Barry. *Male Sexual Awareness*. New York: Carroll and Graf, 1988.

McCarthy, Barry, and Emily McCarthy. *Female Sexual Awareness*. New York: Carroll and Graf, 1989.

Pearsal, Paul. *Super Marital Sex: Loving for Life*. New York: Doubleday, 1987.

Penner, Clifford, and Joyce Penner. *52 Ways to Have Fun, Fantastic Sex*. Nashville: Thomas Nelson, 1993.

————. *Getting Your Sex Life Off to a Great Start: A Guide for Engaged and Newlywed Couples*. Dallas: Word, 1994.

————. *The Gift of Sex*. Dallas: Word, 1981.

————. *Restoring the Pleasure*. Dallas: Word, 1993.

————. *Sex Facts for the Family*. Dallas: Word, 1992.

Penner, Joyce, and Clifford Penner. *Counseling for Sexual Disorders*. Dallas: Word, 1990.

Peterson, Eugene H. *The Message of the New Testament in Contemporary English*. Colorado Springs: NavPress, 1993.

Schnarch, David M. *Constructing the Sexual Crucible: An Integration of Sexual and Marital Therapy*. New York: Norton, 1991.

Seven Promises of a Promise Keeper. Colorado Springs: Focus on the Family, 1994.

Smalley, Gary. *Making Love Last Forever*. Dallas: Word, 1996.

Smalley, Gary, and John Trent. *The Language of Love.* Colorado Springs: Focus on the Family, 1988.

Smedes, Lewis B. *The Art of Forgiving: When You Need to Forgive and Don't Know How.* Nashville: Moorings, 1996.

———. *Forgive and Forget: Healing the Hurts We Don't Deserve.* San Francisco: Harper & Row, 1984.

———. *Love Within Limits: Realizing Selfless Love in a Selfish World.* Grand Rapids, Mich.: Eerdmans, 1978.

Trent, John. *Go the Distance: The Making of a Promise Keeper.* Colorado Springs: Focus on the Family, 1996.

Warren, Neil C. *Finding the Love of Your Life: Ten Principles for Choosing the Right Marriage Partner.* Colorado Springs: Focus on the Family, 1992.

———. *Make Anger Your Ally: Harnessing One of Your Most Powerful Emotions.* Colorado Springs: Focus on the Family, 1992.

———. *The Triumphant Marriage.* Colorado Springs: Focus on the Family, 1995.

Williams, Warwick. *Rekindling Desire: Bringing Your Sexual Relationship Back to Life.* Oakland, Calif.: New Harbinger, 1988.

Zilbergeld, Bernie. *The New Male Sexuality.* New York: Bantam, 1992.

PENNER BOOKS & TAPES

300 North Lake Avenue, Suite 1111A
Pasadena, CA 91101
Telephone: (818) 449-2525 Fax: (818) 564-1250

If you can't find one of our products at your local bookstore, you may order it by using the following form:

Number of Copies   **Total**

_____ *The Gift of Sex.* A general handbook on sexuality for
married couples of all stages and ages. $12.95 _____

_____ *Sex Facts for the Family.* A reference book to help
singles, couples, and parents with sexual decisions
and communication. $12.95 _____

_____ *Getting Your Sex Life Off to a Great Start.* A book
to prepare engaged and newly married couples for a
life of exhilaration and mutual sex. $12.95 _____

_____ *Restoring the Pleasure.* A complete self-help program
to help couples overcome sexual barriers. $12.95 _____

_____ *52 Ways to Have Fun, Fantastic Sex.* One Suggestion
per week to add spark to married sex. $7.95 _____

_____ *Counseling for Sexual Desorders.* For professionals
who help couples find sexual fulfillment. $17.95 _____

_____ *The Magic and Mystery Sex.* Four video hours of
Penner presentation and interviews of couples bring
new openness and joy to sex in marriage. 4 videos $79.95 _____

         Video 1: *The Art of Making Love*
         Video 2: *Discoveries Uniquely Hers*
         Video 3: *His Struggles*
         Video 4: *Keeping the Spark Alive*

_____ *Enjoying the Gift of Sex Seminar* (Call for cassette and
seminar information.)

                                      Subtotal _____
                      (CA Sales Only) Sales Tax_____
                          Postage & Handling_____
                                         Total_____

SEND TO:_____
               _____
               _____
               _____

About the Authors

Clifford L. Penner is a clinical psychologist who holds a B.A. from Bethel College in St. Paul, Minnesota, an M.A. in theology from Fuller Theological Seminary, and a Ph.D. from Fuller's Graduate School of Psychology.

Joyce J. Penner is a clinical nurse specialist, with an emphasis on psychosomatic disorders, who holds a B.S. in nursing from the University of Washington and a master's degree in nursing from UCLA.

The Penners are recognized internationally as sex therapists, educators, and authors. In addition to their full-time sex therapy practice in Pasadena, California, and conducting sexual enhancement seminars, they have written *The Gift of Sex: A Couple's Guide to Sexual Fulfillment; Sex Facts for the Family: A Family Handbook on Sexuality; Restoring the Pleasure: Complete Step-by-Step Programs to Help Couples Overcome the Most Common Sexual Barriers; 52 Ways to Have Fun, Fantastic Sex; Counseling for Sexual Disorders;* and *Getting Your Sex Life Off to a Great Start.*